HIDDEN
HISTORY
of
FRANKLIN COUNTY
VERMONT

HIDDEN
HISTORY
of
FRANKLIN COUNTY
VERMONT

Jason Barney

THE
History
PRESS

Published by The History Press
Charleston, SC
www.historypress.com

Front cover: reproduced with permission of the Swanton Historical Society.
Back cover: courtesy of the Swanton Historical Society.

First published 2021

ISBN 9781540247506

Library of Congress Control Number: 2021931129

Notice: The information in this book is true and complete to the best of our knowledge. It is offered without guarantee on the part of the author or The History Press. The author and The History Press disclaim all liability in connection with the use of this book.

This book is for my wife, Christine. For my writing, she has thankfully helped out as a beta reader. She always understands what I am trying to say, sometimes better than I have written it. Without her love, support and grammar skills, this book would not have been possible.

CONTENTS

CONTENTS

ACKNOWLEDGEMENTS

I'd like to thank the folks at The History Press for giving me another shot at exploring local history. In my first book, *Northern Vermont and the War of 1812*, I was allowed to play in their sandbox, and I am honored to be back. Its publication gave me several opportunities to go into "nerd mode," and I appreciate it. Many thanks go out to everyone who supported that first venture. I'd like to thank all of the Franklin County town historical societies for opening their doors. Thanks go out to fellow author Mark Bushnell, who broke ground with his *Hidden History of Vermont*. My family has been incredibly supportive and interested in these projects. Special acknowledgement goes to members of the MVU staff, who helped me out of several technical problems. They are Rich Ballard, Josh Bourdeau and Sylvia Gagne. The creative people who supported my writing are Armand Messier, Lindsay Didio, Ashley Bowen, Josh Sinz and Diane Mock. On a personal level, educators are only as good as the material used in class. For history teachers, images allow us to deliver historical content better. I want to thank many of my colleagues at Missisquoi Valley Union High School for taking interest in my career. An administrator, Jenn DeSorgher, and a fellow teacher, Julie Curtis, showed up at my door during one of my study halls. They asked to see me in the hall, and I thought they needed use of my height to hang something. When we got outside the classroom, they were smiling and proud. They had nominated me for the Victor R. Swenson Award with the Vermont Humanities Council. They let me know that I had won, that I had been named as the 2019 recipient. Pride and joy showed in their eyes.

ACKNOWLEDGEMENTS

What do you do when someone does something like this for you? I have thanked them many times.

And it continued. Last fall, I was selected by the administration at MVU as the nominee for VFW Teacher of the Year. It was really nice to be thought of in that way. I love history and would not trade teaching students in the classroom for anything. Due to the time and effort of the people mentioned above, you get that in these pages. Special thanks go out to the administration, staff, families and students at Missisquoi Valley Union High School, my place of work. I am proud to be one of you.

HOW THE PRESENT HIDES THE PAST

I n preparing this book, much thought went into how items or topics become hidden. It was an interesting exercise. There are dozens of metaphors for how things become obscure. It was fun defining the shades of gray in what we see or don't see. Franklin County, Vermont, has been inhabited for longer than most people know. People settled along the shores of Lake Champlain thousands of years before Christianity arrived on the scene. Even if European settlement is the measure, there are still very few places in America that have a longer history than here. Samuel de Champlain was exploring our lake before the Pilgrims arrived in Massachusetts Bay.

With this knowledge, some choices needed to be made. Before any writing or research could happen, I had to pick a select group of "worthy" topics. So, an indirect apology is necessary. The book doesn't even come close to covering everything that has ever happened here. The History Press is onto something with this topic, as there are countless local history mysteries to be rediscovered, brought into the public consciousness and enjoyed. Imagine all of the information about the past that can be gleaned from family histories, oral traditions, town history books, churches, cemeteries, old photo albums, yearbooks…the list goes on and on.

The past does not have to remain hidden. At Missisquoi Valley Union High School, where I teach, one of the themes explored in my Abenaki and Local History class is that northwestern Vermont has more "dust in the attic" when compared to most places. Much work has gone into correcting the mistaken view that this area is insignificant, that this area "is not the center of the universe." This may be a sensitive topic for some, and an entire book could be written just on the previous sentence. The truth is that we have a more exciting history than most places in the United States. The hidden history of this county is more nuanced, more layered and more complex than most residents believe.

It has been a busy few years. My previous book, *Northern Vermont and the War of 1812*, came out in August 2019. It was the culmination of a lot of research and history. It was a treat to be able to publish something historically worthy about the area where I was born and raised.

I think I am most proud when one of my students brings up that book. I love my job. Being paid to teach history in my hometown has been a unique experience. I imagine it is a rare person who has enjoyed their job more than I have enjoyed mine. The student-teacher dynamic is so unique. Over the course of a semester, a professional educator will try any number of ways to delivery history content: joking about it, readings, singing, visiting locations, handling artifacts. Well, my first book came out, and some students wanted to talk about the writing process. Other students wanted to talk about the War of 1812. Not all of them, but enough.

If the publication of a book helped my 2019–20 start off great, history in general made it the most rewarding of my career. I was honored to replace Ron Kilburn as president of the Swanton Historical Society. Ron had been president for decades. He wanted to be involved but no longer desired to be the leader. I can only to try to fill his shoes.

With many things, it just helps to ask questions. I had been lucky enough to have college professors with a true love of history, and we had initiated several archaeological digs in search of the barracks from the War of 1812 that had been burned in Swanton in the summer of 1813. High school students helped out with those digs. It was wonderful. I wanted those digs to continue. I mean, I knew it was impossible to have an archaeological dig every year, but I thought that maintaining a relationship with the people "in the know" was a good idea.

I contacted the Vermont Archaeological Society and initiated what has become an open and beneficial relationship. These are incredibly smart people who have dedicated their lives to a very specific "science-y" part of history. They are really nice people. One of their members, Angela Labrador, came up to Swanton and received my War of 1812 pitch, and the search for the barracks is still in the works.

Much of this book will be chronological. However, a few of the topics are so broad that the time periods covered overlap with other eras. Also, a lot of this work will focus on individual towns, but a few are vast enough that they encompass various locations in the county.

I want to encourage you to try to remember back to your childhood. The rivers and creeks where you got your new shoes wet, upsetting Mom and Dad. The accidents and injuries and trips to the doctor. Remember the sound of crinkling wrapping paper at Christmas and birthdays. Remember that smell of a young puppy or the painful red scratches when you took playing with the cat too far. Recall the taste of meals at Thanksgiving, summer get-togethers or family gatherings. Try to isolate the sound of your grandparents' voices. Bring their loving faces into your mind's eye. Hold on to all of these.

Now imagine historians having the opportunity to record all of that information.

Having grown up in Franklin County…that is what writing this book was like.

CHAPTER ONE

ABENAKI SETTLEMENT, HIDDEN BY TIME

O ur indigenous history is quite vast, and much of it will remain hidden forever. European exploration of northwestern Vermont began in the early 1600s. The first Frenchmen to sail the waters of Missisquoi Bay, to hunt beaver pelts or to harvest timber in the Champlain Valley did so about four hundred years ago. The very first European family groups to cross the Atlantic arrived about thirteen or fourteen generations ago.

The Native American presence goes back about twelve thousand years or longer.[1] They saw the last of the glaciers retreat northward. To put things into perspective, if a meter stick were used to measure units of time and occupational lengths, European settlement would account for about three or four centimeters. The Abenaki, the tribe indigenous to this area, and their ancestors would occupy more than nine and a half meters.

That is a lot of undocumented, hidden history.

Academics and archaeologists have broken down this period of Vermont's history into three eras, each with specific time spans. The Paleo period was the earliest, when people survived in an inhospitable, semi-frozen wasteland. The first people probably followed food sources into the region about 9000 BC. As they followed the caribou and the mastodon, the nearly two-mile-thick Laurentian Glacier covering the area was in the process of melting.[2] Historians mark the end of this era at about 6500 BC.

The middle period of Native American occupation is the Archaic, and it spanned slightly more than five thousand years.[3] Evidence suggests extensive trade networks with other groups across North America.

An Abenaki hunting with an atlatl. *Artwork by Ashley Bowen.*

The most recent era, the Woodland, is the least hidden by the past. Franklin County's association with this time is tantalizing, mysterious and so close that it can almost be touched.

Historians break the vast Woodland era into three segments. The Early Woodland encompasses the period leading up to the birth of Christ. The Middle Woodland was the one thousand or so years after that. The Late Woodland measures from about AD 1000 until the first French explorers arrived almost five hundred years ago.

Like children seized by stories of pirates and hidden treasure, professional archaeologists have conducted many digs all over Franklin County and the Champlain Valley that have tried to define the scope of the Native occupation. Children use their imagination and conjures piles of gold and silver coins. The archaeologists have discovered information worth far more than gold and silver, and the public can now reconstruct vast pieces of Native occupation.

It appears that during the Woodland, the early Abenaki began a shift away from hunting and gathering. Earlier peoples were not linked to specific areas and followed food sources to stay alive. That changed about one or two thousand years ago.[4] Several aspects of Native American lifestyle added to the changing way of life. There is a fairly large body of evidence that agriculture developed in warmer climates and then spread to the Northeast.

Sharpened animal bones, handmade pottery, jewelry and other items of value were part of a trade network that included seed varieties that might grow in the Northeast.[5]

The Abenaki settled along waterways for obvious reasons. They did not have to expend a lot of energy to get food, and such places offered access to trade routes. In Franklin County, the prime locations were along Lake Champlain and the shores of the Missisquoi River. These two bodies of water converge in Swanton, where the river empties into Missisquoi Bay, the northeastern most section of Lake Champlain. Previous generations found these areas populated with wild animals. As seeds became available, this area offered fertile soil for growing crops.

Strains of squash were likely the first crop to be harvested and cultivated.[6] There has been no direct evidence (yet) that squash was grown along the banks of the Missisquoi River, but archaeologists have found very old squash seeds as far northeast as Maine.[7]

Not long after, bean seeds were traded and grown.[8] While there is still no direct evidence that they were grown in Swanton, they sure were close. Across the Missisquoi Bay Bridge, in Alburgh, lies the Bohannon Site, where archaeologists found definitive bean seed fragments.[9] This documented evidence suggests that beans were a staple in the Alburgh, Swanton and Highgate areas. The specific types of beans remain a mystery, but traditions suggest that Vermont Cranberry, Jacob's Cattle, Skunk and other varieties have probably been grown on the banks of the Missisquoi River for at least one thousand years.[10]

Finally, about one thousand years ago, corn made its way into the area.[11] The presence of corn was well documented by the first European explorers. There is considerable evidence from Canadian digs, sites throughout New England and some local sites that corn was a very important crop about six hundred years before the first Whites arrived. The Bohannon Site in Alburgh once again provided a gold mine of evidence, but in 2016, the banks of the Missisquoi River in Swanton confirmed what most archaeologists and Abenaki were already well aware of. The picturesque Franklin County cornfield didn't originate with the hardworking old farmer. The first corn wasn't harvested with a tractor. It was grown and used by the Abenaki. Professionals were able to document that corn had been grown when they found corncob remains in pits along the Missisquoi.[12] Some historians are attempting to learn if the local population grew the corn, beans and squash via the "Three Sisters" method. This method has been identified with other tribes, and it may have been used in Vermont. If so, the corn was planted in the center of a mound. As the corn stalks reached for the sun, the beans and squash were planted in a rough circle in and around the mounds. The bean vines snaked up the corn stalks, and the large squash leaves cut down on the weeding and workload in the garden. There is evidence that sunflowers or other plants may have been harvested as well.[13]

The history is not limited to one location. The Missisquoi Wildlife National Refuge hosts numerous known and countless unknown Abenaki sites, all documenting the intense occupation before Whites arrived.

In the last twenty years, the archaeological remains of structures have been discovered. In 2000, what remained of the posts for a longhouse and probable wigwams were uncovered across the bay in the soil in Alburgh. The recent work on the Refuge Site in Swanton revealed the posts molds for another longhouse and smaller structures that were likely wigwams.

What happened when Whites interacted with Native Americans in the 1600s and 1700s is fairly well known. While smallpox, the flu and other diseases were deadly realities in Europe, indigenous populations had no natural immunity. The diseases took hold in coastal villages and then spread

The remains of longhouses have been discovered in Alburgh and Swanton. *Artwork by Lindsay DiDio.*

like wildfire. Wars between France and England spilled over into the North American colonies, and lands were claimed in the name of kings who lived an ocean away. White colonists pushed into Native American areas, and history has recorded the rest.

The region's indigenous people were nearly wiped out by diseases. What they had achieved, how they lived, even who they were had been hidden by time and cultural hegemony.

Today, things are changing. Historians have dug into the past. The Abenaki have worked to claim their heritage and have shared much of their history.

Efforts to maintain Abenaki culture have been embraced by the descendants of Native families. The Abenaki Tribal Headquarters in Swanton fosters cultural renewal. Numerous families have investigated and confirmed their Abenaki lineage.

In late 2020, on the town green in Swanton, an Abenaki totem was erected to honor their history and culture. As time passes, the enduring Native American presence is appropriately no longer hidden away.

CHAPTER TWO

YOU WOULD BE SURPRISED WHAT HAPPENED HERE

Swanton and the Revolution

N otable historical happenings end up being defined as watershed events. There have been plenty of them in America as part of the nation's story. Two hundred fifty years ago, Americans were fed up with England's monarchy, and the Revolutionary War was boiling up on the East Coast.

American school kids review the stories of George Washington and the Founding Fathers. They learn about key flashpoints, like Valley Forge, Bunker Hill and Lexington and Concord. These events were critical to the development of the United States but happened somewhere else. When Vermont schoolchildren learned about the struggle between the colonists and the redcoats, they were asked to imagine far-off forts and battlefields.

Not anymore.

Northern Franklin County has an extensive hidden history with the Revolution.

A lot of it was anchored in Swanton, but there are also nuggets from other towns. Swanton's link originates from a time when it was referred to as Prattsburgh, when New York's claim to the Green Mountains was equal to New Hampshire's.[14] New York probably had the better claim, but Benning Wentworth, the governor of New Hampshire, started chartering towns along the eastern shores of Lake Champlain.

People from New York had already settled in some locations; one of these was along the Missisquoi River. In Prattsburgh, Simon Metcalf set up a sawmill in the early 1770s on the site of the original French settlement.

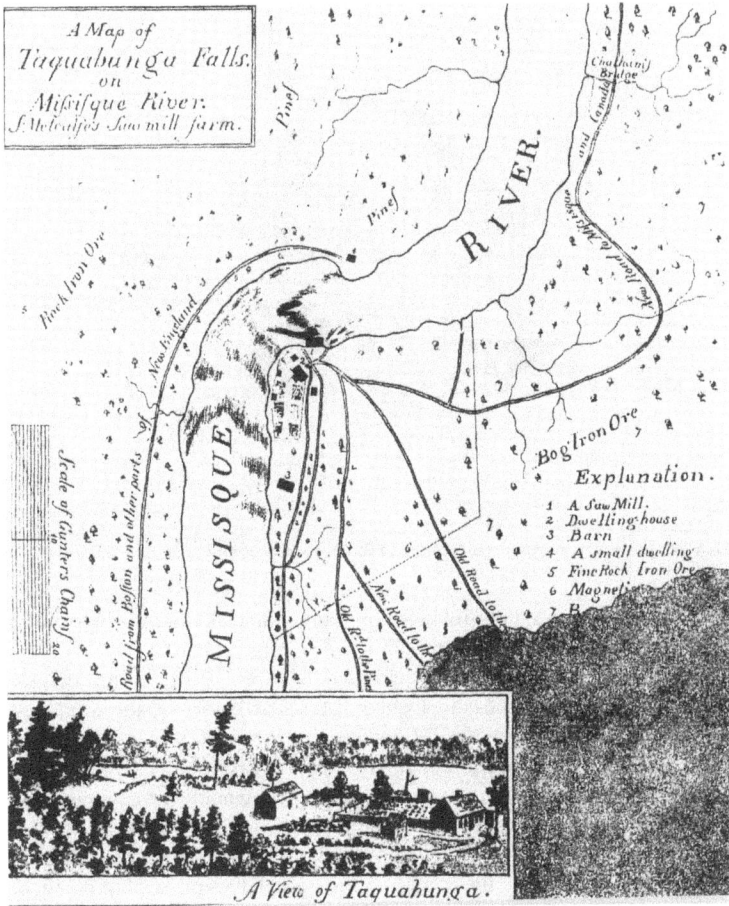

Metcalf's settlement in Swanton in the early 1770s. *Image reproduced courtesy of the Swanton Historical Society.*

Cutting trees required a lot of manual labor, but it is not known how many workers he employed. He also set up a trading post at the very tip of the Missisquoi River delta, where the river opens into Lake Champlain's Missisquoi Bay. He bartered with Abenaki families and had extensive trade networks with the English-controlled French settlements to the north. The

Metcalf's sawmill in Swanton, early in the Revolutionary War. *Artwork by Ashley Bowen.*

land where he set up shop still bears his name, Metcalf's Island.[15] He is also linked to Metcalf's Pond in Fairfield.

After the Revolutionary War erupted in April 1775, events quickly creeped north. Lexington and Concord, the first battles of the war, were fought northwest of Boston in Massachusetts. Just a few weeks later, Ethan Allen and the Green Mountain Boys plotted to take Fort Ticonderoga at the southern tip of Lake Champlain. Benedict Arnold, with semi-official authority within the colonial army, inserted himself into those plans. Fort Ticonderoga was taken in May, and for the next few weeks, the fledgling colonial effort to expel the British from Lake Champlain played out in Franklin County's backyard.

Metcalf's sawmill and trading post were tucked deep along Missisquoi Bay, on the northeast shoulder of the lake. Benedict Arnold snuck north to St. Jean, seized the British naval ship there and retreated. Ethan Allen was a bit tardy and, with a small band of Green Mountain Boys, tried to capture and hold St. Jean. One night later, he retreated back along the Richelieu River. While primary source documentation is scarce, during these critical early months of the war, Metcalf's sawmill was likely visited by scouts from both sides.[16]

However, the historical documentation is clearer as spring transitioned to summer. Arnold moved the small American fleet up and down Lake Champlain, keeping an eye on the mouth of the Richelieu River, just north of Isle La Motte and west of Alburgh. The Americans were preparing an invasion of Quebec, and they needed all of the information they could get.

A spy mission was conceived. Bayze Wells and Major John Brown were sent north to evaluate the British presence at Isle aux Noix and St. Jean.[17] They traveled the northern part of the lake by canoe and snuck into Quebec on foot to avoid detection. They found that the British had done virtually nothing with Isle aux Noix, situated just a few miles north of Metcalf's sawmill. There was, however, a substantial enemy presence at St. Jean. Fearing detection, the men set to return to American-occupied Fort Ticonderoga. They traveled south and east through the Quebec countryside until they came to the Missisquoi River, probably somewhere in Highgate. They followed it westward and came to Metcalf's settlement.[18] There, they procured a canoe from Metcalf and continued south to deliver critical information to Arnold, Allen and the colonial leadership.

The American invasion of Quebec commenced in late August, and the colonial army used Isle La Motte as a jumping point into Canada. As August turned to September, hundreds of American soldiers sailed the lake, just

Early colonial spy mission that went through Swanton. *Artwork by Ashley Bowen.*

west of Metcalf's trading post. During this time, Metcalf likely sold to the colonial army whatever it needed.

Isle aux Noix became the American headquarters as they lay siege to St. Jean, a stepping-stone to capturing Montreal. Lake Champlain was a flurry of activity, as colonial troops in bateaux and gunboats moved north. Metcalf's was the closest active sawmill to the American invasion as it creeped north. Probably not particularly invested in which side won the war, he sold goods and lumber to the American effort.[19] Later, when the British turned the tide, his entanglement with the rebels would prove problematic.

Metcalf's support went beyond supplies. Throughout the campaign to take Quebec, the effort was plagued by organizational problems. One of the biggest was the transport of armies from southern New England to the fighting in Quebec. Lake Champlain was the most obvious route, but plans were in development for a military road between the Connecticut River Valley and the northern edge of Lake Champlain. Metcalf actively communicated with the American leadership, who wanted the road to link Newbury, New Hampshire, and Missisquoi Bay.[20] At different stages of the war, the road was worked on, reaching the eastern spine of the Green Mountains. The planning got as far as Hazen's Notch, near Montgomery, but the successful British defense of Quebec halted these plans.

Metcalf's activities shifted as the British expelled the Americans from Quebec during the spring and summer of 1776. With redcoats deployed along the border, he tried to avoid attention. However, at different points, the Americans took Metcalf and his workmen prisoner. They had come to doubt his real loyalties.[21] The American defense of Fort Ticonderoga and Mount Independence became a priority, and as the troops retreated, orders were given to burn Metcalf's sawmill in Swanton.[22]

Even as the war shifted to areas outside of New England, Metcalf's was still valuable to the Americans. Several German Hessian soldiers, serving alongside the British, had become familiar with the area and abandoned the Crown's army. They defected across the border in August.[23] Metcalf's settlement was a stopover location for these defectors as they made their way south, farther into American lines.

While the British were able to regain Canada, they were not able to push south during 1776. Benedict Arnold and his navy successfully held them off until October, when the royals briefly tiptoed south after the Battle of Valcour Island. Winter was just weeks away, and the British planned a larger invasion for the following year. Through the winter and spring of 1777, the Crown gathered its forces in Canada. Loyalist Americans, a few Native

American tribes and British and Hessian reinforcements all descended on Lake Champlain in the summer of 1777.

The British were now in control of the lake, and they embarked on the Saratoga campaign in an effort to divide the colonies. Johnny Burgoyne took his army into the Hudson River and Lake George regions but was defeated in October. They retreated back through the Champlain Valley, into Canada, and Metcalf had to continue a difficult balancing act with his allegiances through the end of 1777 and most of 1778.

In 1778, the British conducted raids south into New York and the Green Mountains. Using the lake, they pushed as far south as Fort Ticonderoga again, but the intent was not to seize the fort. They wanted to wreak havoc on the New Hampshire grants and hit patriot communities in the Champlain Valley. During these incursions, they torched anything that could be used by rebels, including blockhouses, homes and sawmills.[24]

Metcalf was taken prisoner by the British and jailed in Montreal. As the war came to an end, there was still British activity just north of the border during 1780 and 1781. Metcalf was released and returned to his settlement, but the circumstances along the frontier had drastically changed. The first American colonists were scouting the area, and the British still maintained a blockhouse just south of his settlement, in North Hero. The Allen family, whose fingerprints and agents were all over most parts of Vermont, had finally moved into the Missisquoi area by the early 1780s. Metcalf had to go to court to dispute their new claim and ultimately lost. He left the area not long afterward.

The 250th anniversary of the American Revolution will be celebrated in a few years. With it, historians are making a broader effort to reexamine the conventional stories about Vermont's Revolutionary War history. Scholarship is appropriately investigating the roles of African Americans, Native Americans and women in the struggle to define early America. As research uncovers more, location and place should also be an important lens through which history is studied. The stories of small towns, small places and little-known people are just as important as those of the heroes elevated by history books. That is certainly true of Swanton's Revolutionary War history.

CHAPTER THREE

"WE THOUGHT WE SAID GOODBYE"

The Tories Along the Border

P art of the local lore in the town of Highgate is that some of the first settlers thought they were putting down roots in Canada. It is a claim a lot of people have heard about but few actually know the origin of. Like so many historical topics, the truth is hidden in the details....

In the lead-up to 1775, the land in question was essentially the frontier between Native Americans, Quebec and the thirteen colonies. The exact border wasn't as precise as today, because eighteenth-century mapping can't compare to satellite measurements. The border was the frontier because it was so far away from Montreal and Quebec City, New York City and Boston.

The Revolution changed all of that.

What had been a far-off contested area between two armies became available for settlement. From 1775 to 1781, the land changed hands multiple times, with raids and skirmishes all throughout the region. The American victory at Saratoga changed the lines on the map. The Tories—Americans loyal to England—found that northern Lake Champlain and the "Hampshire Grants" was the best route to get away from the rebellious colonies. With the recognition that England may not crush the rebellion, over five hundred Tory military men and their families fled over Lake Champlain to Quebec.[25]

It was some of these people who first settled northwestern Franklin County, principally parts of Highgate that bordered Canada. It didn't happen overnight. Loyalist units were part of the British army in Quebec throughout 1778 and 1779. During this time, soldiers sent word to their

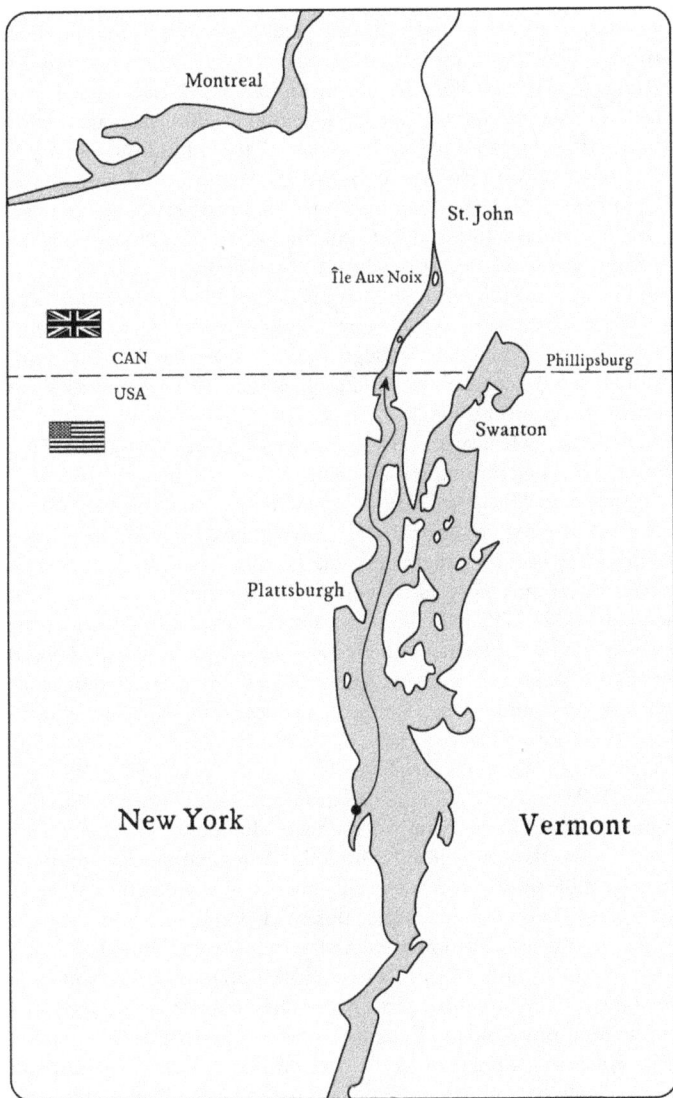

After the Revolutionary War, Loyalists left the colonies for Canada. *Artwork by Lindsay DiDio.*

families in the thirteen colonies making arrangements for their new homes in Canada. The New York legislature passed laws giving those families a short time to remove themselves from the land they had owned in that colony.[26] Loyalists from the Green Mountains also evacuated north.[27] In many cases, they traveled under a flag of truce to Crown Point, New York, stopped at Point Au Fer just across the lake from Alburgh and then traveled north to St. Jean, Quebec.[28] New York was very active in pushing out Loyalist families. In July 1780, at a time when the fighting had shifted away from New England, Tory wives and families were essentially forced out. In the area of Hoosick, at least nine families were prompted to depart. By October of the same year, more families in the region were forced to move north.[29] There was enough nonmilitary-related traffic that the British deemed it necessary to build a blockhouse at Dutchman's Point in North Hero to protect them.[30]

Additionally, the British and Loyalist presence during 1776 and 1777 near the border had been substantial. When the war ended, many of the expelled immediately saw Missisquoi Bay as a new home. Some in the Canadian government wanted to resettle the refugees farther west, near the St. Lawrence River, but the attention of the Loyalists returned to the territory they had fought over just years before.[31] The Revolutionary War officially came to an end in 1783. Not long after, the first request to settle Missisquoi Bay was made by the former Americans.[32] They were originally housed in a barracks at St. Jean. As early as August 30, 1783, former members of the "Loyal Rangers" and "Kings Rangers" petitioned to settle the area north and east of Missisquoi Bay.

The petition went unanswered.

In late 1783 and early 1784, small groups of families decided to ignore the Quebec government. Many of the men who fought in these units had patrolled, worked, occupied or scouted the American border. It had clear water, accessible land and was virtually absent of any French settlers. The prime location had future economic potential. Timber and other products could be moved up and down the water routes to Montreal. By March 1, 1784, English authorities received reports that Loyalist families had ignored the resettlement orders.[33] The families had instead moved into the border region, probably in Highgate, approximately three miles south of the Pike River in Canada, along the banks of Rock River. Two individuals were specifically mentioned in reports prepared for the British government in Canada. Captain Meyers was clearing a substantial amount of land to raise a thousand bushels of corn. Captain Ruiter was in the area using his

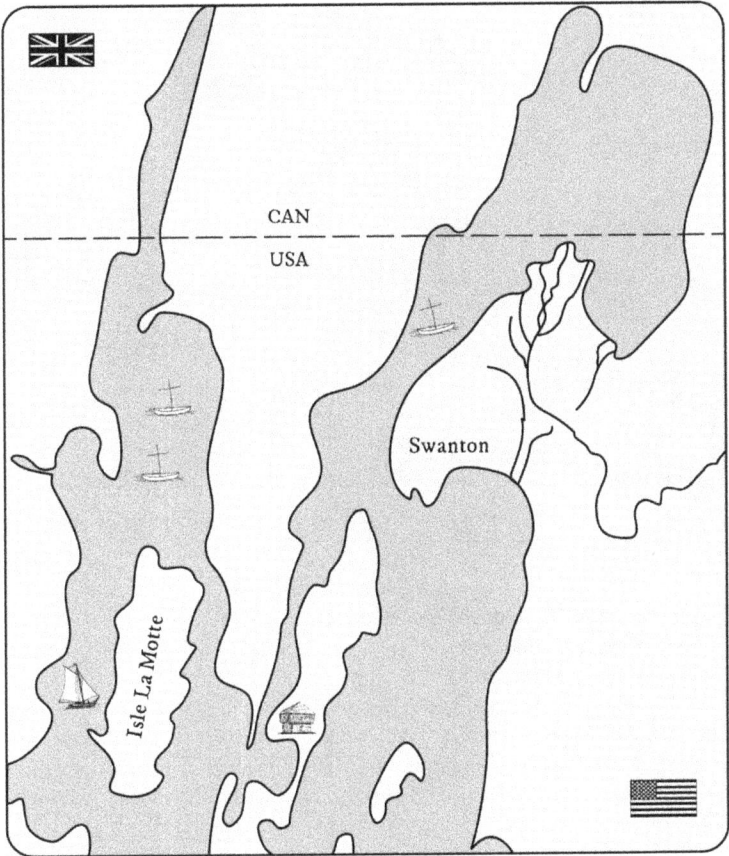

Missisquoi Bay became an attractive location for Americans who favored the Crown.
Artwork by Lindsay DiDio.

oxen to clear land as well. Another report indicated that there were nine families living or preparing homes "north of the line," and there were another thirteen men working for those families. Other individuals who defied the British provincial government were former Loyalist soldiers Christian Wehr and Azariah Pritchard. The "line" being referred to was the forty-fifth parallel, which was used to mark the border between Quebec and the American states. The era's surveying was at best imprecise, and the

View of Missisquoi Bay. This area may have been first settled by the Loyalists leaving for Quebec. *Photo by Armand Messier and Northern Vermont Aerial Photography.*

maps were understandably vague. More than two hundred years of history show that the international border is about a mile farther *north* of where the families may have settled.

By October 1784, over 5,600 Loyalists and their families had left the former colonies. This number was significant enough that it represented nearly 5 percent of the population of Quebec. The resettlement plans were an organizational nightmare, and settling land near the former colonies was not desirable.[34]

What complicated the situation were assumptions about the location of the border and the paths of the Missisquoi and Rock Rivers. If the Missisquoi Loyalists had their way, they would claim the land between the forty-fifth parallel and the rivers.[35] This was more than problematic for the British government, as most of this land, now encompassing the towns of Highgate and Swanton, was commonly agreed to be within the range of the old New Hampshire Grants.

Rather than get the small group under control, the British government learned that settlement of Missisquoi Bay had ramped up. Subjects of the Crown were settling dangerously close to land they had just been kicked out of. Complicating things more, the territory on the east side of the bay was already inhabited. John Hilliker, the first American colonist to settle in Swanton, was just a few miles south of Rock River.[36] The Abenaki were living in wigwams on the east bank of the Missisquoi River. Throughout the 1780s, families, including the Butterfields, Wagoners, Lampmans, Hogles and Asselestynes, put down roots near the Missisquoi. Some historical texts suggest that a few of these American colonial settlers were actually farther north and east, in present-day Highgate, and very close to the Loyalists.[37] Some of this group may have been ex-Loyalists as well but not associated with those in Quebec.

As the British investigated the situation, they sent agents to find out how many families had defied their wishes. What they found did not please them. The Ruiter family had built two homes. The Best family was in the process of cutting wood for a house. The Hyatts were building. The Mocks had built a hut and were preparing land for farming. They were a short distance from Rock River, less than three miles inland from Missisquoi Bay. Other families were in the area, but construction had not yet begun on their homes. The British government determined that, due to the swampy terrain, it would be nearly impossible to send a contingent of the military to physically remove them.[38] The government cut off rations and supplies to the troublesome

Loyalists arrive in Missisquoi Bay. *Artwork by Ashley Bowen.*

squatters.[39] Muddying the waters even more was a letter from the Missisquoi Loyalists that argued they had really settled on "Indian Lands" not owned by the king, so there wasn't a problem. Compounding the issue further, they spread word to other groups, attracting the interest of a small segment of Quebec's French population. French families settled in the border zone, very near the Missisquoi Loyalists, as early as 1786.[40] Christian Wehr, one of the defiant settlers, was involved with the settlement of Phillipsburg, Quebec, just to the north of Highgate, along Missisquoi Bay.[41]

The British government was more interested in working with the Loyalists, who would willingly depart, than in spending resources dealing with troublemakers. Most of the other Loyalists followed the edicts of the British government and accepted resettlement in the suggested locations.

For those who settled in the shade of gray between the present forty-fifth parallel and the international border, the struggle for land wasn't quite over yet. Within Quebec, land was organized as small agricultural fiefdoms. When the ownership of St. Armand, Quebec, changed hands, it was discovered that the Loyalists along Rock River had never legally purchased the land. They were forced to buy it through the appropriate local authorities in St. Armand after having lived on it for close to a decade.

The original occupiers of the land, the Abenaki, figured prominently in the situation as the 1780s ended and the 1790s began. The early land agreements had effectively been used to carve up lots, first by the French and English, then by the colonists in the area. The Abenaki returned to their homelands from faraway hunting trips, and the situation became more complicated. Native bands fished on the lake and hunted on the banks of the Missisquoi throughout the 1780s. Abenaki land was taken by American colonists in Swanton and by British Loyalists in Quebec. Tension boiled over when a group of Abenaki appeared in the village of Swanton, threatening to burn the settlers out of their homes and kill the cattle.[42] A point of history that remains hidden is the possibility that Missisquoi Loyalists brought slaves with them from Upstate New York.[43] In the late 1700s, slavery was still legal. Local lore in St. Armand suggests that some of the first settlers did in fact have slaves and that there was a cemetery for them near the international border.

In 1791, the first official U.S. census put Highgate's population at 103 people. There were 17 heads of families listed. Many of these had Dutch or German surnames, further confirmation that the area's first permanent white settlers were probably from the Hudson River Valley of New York.[44] Many of them were probably expelled Loyalists seeking a new home.

CHAPTER FOUR

"FIGHTING TO THE NORTH"

Violence in Quebec Spills over the Border

It's weird for most Vermonters to realize that Canada experienced revolutions. It is even more interesting to learn that the northern tier of Franklin County towns became a de facto refuge for those plotting change in Canada.

One of the rebellions in question happened in the late 1830s. The tensions involved were multigenerational and started when the British seized Quebec at the end of the French and Indian Wars, in the 1750s and 1760s. The English struggled to govern the local French Canadian population. Most of the occupiers were English Protestants; the original French settlers were Catholic. There were cultural differences about governing and land ownership. The English in Quebec were still loyal to their king but were influenced by years of small-town government and property ownership from the American colonies. In Canada, a more feudal system remained; smaller individual farms were part of larger estates. Tensions over how the English-speaking minority governed the French majority never went away. For the most part, the French accepted the reality of English rule. Every few years, tensions erupted, and radical elements of French society tried to overthrow the Englishmen.

Events came to a head in the late 1830s. The crop yields had been weak, which put the small, agrarian French communities in a desperate situation. Potato harvests were poor in successive years. Wheat was damaged or destroyed by early frosts, and some communities turned to eating farm horses to get by.[45] This fostered a movement led by Louis-Joseph Papineau, a push for French Canadian independence. Revolutionary ideas ran so deep that possible annexation by the United States seemed a better fate than dealing with the Englishmen.[46] It didn't help that Queen Victoria, who was only seventeen, ascended to the throne of England in the late summer of 1837, just as revolutionary leanings gripped the countryside.[47]

In October, radicals resorted to acts of violence. November brought more conflict, with open rebellion underway by early December.[48] Along the border, Vermont newspapers reported on the happenings. Some speculated that there would be conflict along Missisquoi Bay as hostilities broke out in communities near Montreal.[49] The early engagements did not go particularly well for the Canadian Patriots, particularly along the Richelieu River. Speculation spread that Papineau and other leaders might have fled across the border into Vermont.[50]

Often, it took a while for news to spread. Days might pass before accounts appeared in the press.

The reports were true, and violent events unfolded before newspapers were able to report on them.

When "the Affair at Moore's Corners" happened, Franklin County was indirectly involved with the Canadian rebellion. The reporting was quite a bit behind actual events. For example, by December 11, the government of Canada had offered a $4,000 reward for Papineau and rebel leaders. They wanted him for crimes committed north of the border, but they weren't even aware of his activities in Vermont.

Papineau had departed Canada and arrived in Swanton as early as late November.[51] Several of his associates traveled south, too, and they had enough men to form a small military unit. They actively sought out Americans with an axe to grind against the British-controlled government. Bands of Canadians were on the Vermont border and hoped the local population would join their cause.

Days later, there were numerous Canadian Patriots in Swanton. Julius Gagnou, one of Papineau's officers, was sent to search the Quebec countryside along the American border for fighting men. On the night of December 5, he returned with eighty-four volunteers.[52]

On the morning of December 6, some of Papineau's group was in the small village of Phillipsburg, Quebec, looting the community.[53] Tipping their hand as to what the objective would be later that day, they redeployed into Vermont and waited for more French Canadian rebels.

Some had secretly been gathering in Swanton for the previous week.

View of the Canadian border from Highgate. *Photo by Armand Messier and Northern Vermont Aerial Photography.*

The violent behavior alerted the Loyalist Canadians. Women and children were ushered away from the area. Small groups patrolled the roads near Missisquoi Bay, where three routes needed to be monitored. The first was the direct road south from Philipsburg, which hugged the shore near the bay, went through Highgate and led to Swanton, about five miles away. Men also patrolled a much shorter road that intersected with Missisquoi Bay. This road is the present-day Rheaume Road. The final possible entrance was near Saxe's Mills, directly south of the Village of St. Armand. The present-day road is Ballard Road. Men from the Canadian hamlets of Pigeon Hill, Bedford and Frelighsburg arrived in the early afternoon, and the Methodist chapel in St. Armand was turned into a base of operations.[54]

Departing Canadian soil, the band of twenty or so agitators passed by the schoolhouse near Missisquoi Bay in Highgate at about 9:00 a.m. They stopped and placed Patriot literature on the schoolhouse door, then proceeded south to link up with their compatriots.[55]

The Canadian Patriots departed Swanton at about 2:00 p.m. Walking over recently fallen snow, they traveled north. Over time, the roads have changed, but they marched along the bay and were monitored by the Loyalists who awaited them.[56] Just as school was getting out for the afternoon, Papineau's men passed by the Highgate schoolhouse again, where they were observed by the young students and the schoolteacher.[57]

It is estimated that about two hundred revolutionaries assembled in the area of Saxe's Mill's in Highgate near sunset. Just a few miles to the north, a hasty defense was underway. Desperate Loyalists had sent word to Isle aux Noix and expected weapons and reinforcements from the English military installation on the Richelieu. During the afternoon, they deployed to the southwest, very close to the border, expecting the Quebec Patriots to cross at Phillipsburg. Based on their advanced location, they were in position to engage the rebels just north of Rheaume Road.[58]

At Saxe's Mill's, the two hundred revolutionaries took stock of their numbers and supplies. They had managed to get their hands on two small cannon, but only one was serviceable. The other one was in bad shape, and they feared deploying it. The ammunition for the big guns was limited. They had 6,000 musket cartridges, which they hoped to disseminate among other radicals who might flock to their cause. They had 112 muskets and 14 iron pikes. The men proudly waved two brand-new revolutionary flags.[59]

Evening darkness settled along the border. Spies and scouts from both sides tried to glean the size and locations of enemy forces. In the hour after dusk, the Patriots received word that government forces awaited them near Philipsburg. A change in plans was made, and through the December night, they marched north along present-day Ballard Road. They organized themselves into three small units. The Loyalists quickly learned of the enemy redeployment. Leaving a small portion of their force near the bay, they moved farther north and east and waited for the rebels on high ground near the present-day four corners in the center of St. Armand village.[60]

Papineau's forces marched into the ambush.

The defenders fired first, surprising and disorienting the radicals in the darkness. As volleys poured into the rebel position, chaos ensued and a few men were wounded. Facing oppressive incoming fire, Patriots desperately tried to get their cannons in place. Retreating men, disorganization and lack of light won out. The Loyalists fired into the area around the road, and more rebels fell. The invaders abandoned their cannons, much of their ammunition and their wounded. Shamed, they skulked back across the Vermont border to lick their wounds.[61]

Sympathies in Franklin County were apparent enough that the president of the United States ordered the military to monitor the situation. With foreign revolutionaries organizing on American soil, the federal government had every right to be concerned. It was not appropriate for the United States

Canadian rebels marching north through Highgate. *Artwork by Ashley Bowen.*

to get involved in internal Canadian affairs, and Papineau and his followers had too much sympathy in Vermont.

In the early months of 1838, a local company of Americans was raised to make sure the nation's neutrality was maintained. It was organized by the U.S. Army at the direction of Lieutenant Miller under the command of General Wool. Some of these men were deployed as far away as Troy, Vermont. Many locals served in this unit. Squads were sent to Alburgh to monitor the situation there. At least one group was deployed to Highgate Falls to intercept supplies being smuggled to Canadian refugees.

The American company was on the border when Canadian Patriots crossed the line at Alburgh. Due to the unknown presence of a large government force just to the north, the French Canadians surrendered near Caldwell's Manor, Quebec. In a bit of international tapdancing, the defeated Canadians were allowed to lay down their arms and return to the United States. The Americans opened ranks, letting the defeated onto U.S. soil. Under military escort, they were brought to St. Albans.[62]

The effects of the radical Canadians on the Vermont border played out for months. An increased military presence remained on the border. Almost a year later, there was an incident at Napierville, Quebec. Just after that was the Battle of Odelltown Church a few miles west of Missisquoi Bay and the Richelieu River. Over fifty French Canadian Patriots were killed and some of their leadership taken prisoner.[63] After these defeats, the rebellion flailed and lost support. Loyalists in Canada maintained forces at Isle aux Noix, and a blockhouse was built in Philipsburg in late 1838. Finished in 1839, it was on elevated ground to monitor the roads from the United States and keep a watchful eye on Missisquoi Bay.[64] Tensions remained high as a few buildings along the border were burned in the spring. This brought a small U.S. presence into the woods of Highgate for a short time.[65]

The Patriot rebellion led many in the frontier communities of Quebec, near the forty-fifth parallel, to reevaluate their allegiances. Not long after, a large number of French Canadian families, unsuccessful in rebellion and frustrated with English rule, migrated south of the border into Highgate and Swanton.[66]

Chapter Five

Some of Our Early Churches

C hurches are full of history. Their structure, windows, size and
architecture give glimpses into the past. They provide insight into
the beliefs of different eras and tell us a lot about early Vermonters
and their relationship with the divine.

Such is the case with Vermont's second-oldest shrine, the Catholic church
built in Swanton in the 1700s. The oldest was the Catholic presence on Isle
La Motte in 1666. Several hundred French soldiers built a fort there, at the
very beginning of the French and Indian Wars. Not much is known about
this structure, especially since it was within a fort over three hundred years
ago. The site became St. Anne's Shrine, still a worship site for Catholics.

The semi-permanent Catholic presence in Swanton arrived in the 1740s.
There was extensive interaction between the Frenchmen from Quebec and
the Abenaki. The French cemented their presence on Lake Champlain early
in the 1730s, when they built forts to the south. As their occupation expanded,
they constructed windmills on the coasts of Alburgh and Colchester.

In the 1740s and '50s, Swanton consisted of several wooden cabins, a
sawmill along the Missisquoi River, likely a dock for occasionally boat traffic
and a house of worship. Its Catholic Church was along the east bank of
the Missisquoi River. And it wasn't just for the French. The church was
purposefully established as a mission to convert the Abenaki to Christianity.
While the precise location is not known, it was near the end of present-day
Monument Road. Nothing remains of this building, although it is depicted
on one of the earliest maps from the era.

The old church in the center of Franklin village. *Photo by Armand Messier and Northern Vermont Aerial Photography.*

Swanton has been home to numerous other churches. Their history involves settlement by English American Protestants. Much of the first worship was done in homes by Methodists, Congregationalists and Baptists. The First Congregationalist Church, at the head of the Swanton town green near the Town Clerk's Office, was erected as early as 1822.

The first Methodist gatherings were around 1806, in an old schoolhouse. For decades, the building was shared on and off by the Congregationalists, Episcopalians, Methodists and even a few Quakers. The current church was erected in the center of the village in 1848 and rebuilt in 1886.[67] The Episcopalian church, located at the head of the park and on the edge of Grand Avenue, was built in 1876. The current Catholic Church, the Church of the Nativity, was built in 1925.[68]

Other communities have different timelines and reflect varying levels of settlement. In each town, members of the faith had to have enough settlers to raise funds for a place of worship. In some cases, communities were so new and populations so small, it took decades for churches to be erected.

Bakersfield's religious history is complex. The first settlers arrived in the early 1790s. Small groups and families trickled in for almost a decade before efforts to attract a Christian preacher commenced. There was an initiative to bring in one of the faith, but a "buyer beware" situation developed. After a few town meetings in which the topic came up, a committee was formed to try to bring in the Reverend Samuel Sumner. After some back and forth about appropriate compensation, the reverend did come, and he did minister, but rarely. Even with his presence, as new settlers arrived, residents described the community as having no church. Finally, the First Congregationalists attempted to organize. For brief periods, there were Methodists, Baptists and Universalists but never for periods long enough to remain formally organized. Between 1821 and 1831, several clergy ministered but never stayed. The first house of worship was finally built in 1831 on the east side of the Post Road.[69]

In Berkshire, the first settlers arrived in the early 1790s and put down roots not far from the Missisquoi River. As with so many other hamlets, ministers often arrived well before communities had resources to erect a church. In those early days, at least three preachers settle in town. On occasion, they conducted religious services, but prior to the 1820s, they farmed more than they professed the word of God. That changed in 1821, when the Episcopalian church was erected in East Berkshire and consecrated by Bishop Griswold. One of the first preachers in the area, Jordan Gray, had an accident in the Trout River and drowned. For the next few years, the East Berkshire church was occasionally used by congregations from Montgomery, and for the next few decades, numerous men ministered there. The Congregationalist Church established its presence on the east side of town and as early as 1823 held organized services. Baptists, Universalists and Methodists all contributed to the erection of a Union House in the center of town and shared the building. The Methodists also used a chapel in West Berkshire.[70]

Enosburg too was settled in the mid-1790s. Its religious history started in 1804. A traveling minister, Job Swift of Bennington, became ill while preaching in the village. He died, and his body was buried in the cemetery just north of town. The Universalists also put up a church, probably in the 1840s, which attracted a number of French Canadians. They attended services there until the Catholic church in Enosburg Falls was erected. The Methodists put up a chapel in West Enosburg, probably in 1839. There had been organized religious meetings in various homes and other locations since 1812. A Baptist church was built in Enosburg. In the center of town, the Congregationalists built their first meetinghouse in 1821. Episcopalians built their churches in the center of town as well.[71]

Fairfield's religious history starts with the Congregationalists. In 1805, shortly after the town was settled, the Reverend Jonathan Edwards was assigned to the area. He also ministered in other communities. The Reverends Benjamin Wooster and Nathaniel Turner preached in those early

Berkshire Congregationalist church. This building hosts the Berkshire Historical Society. *Photo by Armand Messier and Northern Vermont Aerial Photography.*

Fairfield Catholic church. *Photo by Armand Messier and Northern Vermont Aerial Photography.*

days. Homes were used for services and prayer until 1840. The Episcopal Church became established in the community when, in 1814, its bishop visited and confirmed thirty people. The church was built in 1815 and had fluctuating membership over the next few decades. The old building was taken down in 1864 and replaced with another, more modern structure the next year. There was a Methodist presence in town, but services were often held in people's houses.[72]

In 1824, the Congregationalists and the Baptists jointly built the first meetinghouse in Fairfax. The two faiths alternated use, until the presence of enough Baptists allowed for the construction of a separate building in 1848. The decades passed, membership went up and down and then the Great Depression hit. The Baptist church fell on hard times, and the Methodists and Baptists combined their worship into the United Church of Fairfield. The Baptist building still stands, and fundraisers are currently underway to try to help pay for the restoration of the building.[73] Catholics came to Fairfax, probably from Westford, just after the American Civil War. No doubt some lived in the area for years but not enough to build a church. That changed in 1872, when the Church of Mary Magdalene was completed. Over time, the name of the parish was changed to St. Luke's; the building is still used today.

The religious history of Fletcher, which was established so far from the settled areas near the lake, started much later than that of many other communities. The first known instance of anyone ministering was a Baptist, Joseph Wilcox, who probably used the town schoolhouse in 1817. The population never expanded greatly, and outside ministers visited the community often. The Union Church was organized in the 1830s. There was a Methodist presence in town around the 1850s, but this was for a short period. The Congregationalists had a small presence between the 1820s and 1860s.[74] In the early days, each of these faiths agreed to occupy and share the Town Meeting House, which was built in 1831.

Franklin's church history is fairly condensed compared to that of other communities. The 1824 Meeting House, located in the center of the present village, lodged four separate denominations. The Universalists, Methodists, Baptists and Congregationalists all used the building as a place of worship until 1845. Afterward, only the Congregationalists used it. The Methodists built their own church, right next door, in 1844. Attendance and religious interest waxed and waned, and by 1921, the structure was under the joint authority of the Methodists and the Congregationalists once again. Shared management worked well for the two denominations. The present Methodist church, built in 1866, was erected on the site of the 1844 structure. In East

Franklin, not far from the Canadian border, a nondenominational church was constructed in the 1860s. The Universalists, Baptists and Methodists all made use of it. While there have been some alterations, it is very much in the same state as when it was built. The Universalists also had their own building near Brown's Corners. The current Catholic church is St. Mary's on Route 120, built in 1916. Over one hundred years old, this building has been repaired and updated a few times.[75]

Georgia has had numerous churches and faiths over time. The first groups were the Congregationalists and the Baptists, who were among the first settlers, in 1792 and 1793. The town charter had provisions for some land to be set aside for a house of worship. Meanwhile, for years, the Baptists had no preacher, but the faithful gathered in the home of Abraham Hathaway. There were seventeen founding members. In 1802, the Old White Meeting House was built, and the Baptists helped pay for it. The Congregationalists and the Baptists haggled over its use until they decided to share it. There weren't enough Methodists until the 1830s, and their place of worship was not erected until 1848. One that no longer exists is the Emmanuel Episcopal Church in East Georgia. Sarah Am Hyde, who taught Sunday school at many different locations for various denominations, collected funds for the house of worship in 1866. The building, constructed in 1871 and 1872, was where thirty-three families and almost 150 individuals practiced their faith. The numbers in the parish declined to 60 members by 1890. By 1942, only 5 people were attending. In 1946, the building was demolished.

Highgate has had multiple churches, and its history is as varied as the early settlers of the area. People came shortly after the end of the American Revolution. Three religious meetinghouses were erected on the north side of the Missisquoi River by Congregationalists, Methodists and Catholics. The Episcopal church is in Highgate Falls, located on the east side of the green. It was built in 1831. The current Methodist church was built in the late 1860s. The impressive brick building still stands near the town center. The first locations of Congregationalist organized teachings were in the northwest portion of town. They met in old schoolhouses until the middle of the 1800s, when the "Little White Church" near Missisquoi Bay was erected. The location of the Catholic churches is related to Highgate's proximity to French Canadian settlements to the north. The first Catholic church was north of Highgate Center and east of Missisquoi Bay, just a few miles from the Canadian border. At some point, the building was moved to Highgate Center. The current Catholic church, St. Louis Parish on Lampkin Street, is the third location of Catholic worship.[76]

The Methodist church located in Highgate Center. *Photo by Armand Messier and Northern Vermont Aerial Photography.*

Saint Bartholomew's Church in Montgomery. This beautiful building is the home of the town's historical society. *Photo by Armand Messier and Northern Vermont Aerial Photography.*

Montgomery, one of the final areas to be settled in Franklin County, has a shorter religious history than most of the other communities. The first Episcopal visitations happened in the early 1820s, as the location hadn't attracted enough settlers for a permanent meetinghouse. The schoolhouse and private homes were used early on. The Episcopalians, the first to organize, constructed their church in 1835. Over time, membership increased and slight alterations were made. In 1849, the building was repainted and new shingles were placed on the roof. In 1850, the size of the congregation was about one hundred participants. In 1890, the Union Church building received a new name, St. Bartholomew's. This impressive structure has been renovated a few times and stands in the center of town.[77] There were enough Congregationalists to build a church in 1841. The Methodists erected their house of worship in 1843. The Baptists first organized around 1820, but due to relatively low numbers, they worshiped at different locations. It took four decades until the congregation was large enough to support a building. By the middle of the 1860s, work had begun on it. By the late 1860s, they were enjoying the fruits of their labor and praying in their own house of God. This structure still stands in Montgomery Center.[78] The Catholic presence arrived a bit later than the other faiths. Saint Isidore's Catholic Church was put up in 1881, but there were smaller Masses and ceremonies dating back as early as 1855. Over the decades, the building received periodic upgrades, but in 1959, it was restored to its historic condition. The church is also located in Montgomery Center.

Richford's religious history is that of a frontier town. As far as early ministers went, the townspeople took what they could get. Ministers always traveled through; if the locals were lucky, they might get the attention of one of these travelers. Shortly after 1800, the first school went up, which was a log cabin on present-day Pinnacle Road. It was occasionally used as a meetinghouse. A fire consumed it; not long after, a replacement was built. These buildings were occasionally used as houses of worship. In 1802, a Methodist minister gave sermons in homes of different settlers. At the same time, Baptists were able to attract a minister from Quebec.[79] Richford's first church was built in the 1840s. There were a few different groups of Baptists around, but they jointly agreed on the construction of a house of worship in 1842. It featured some brick but was mostly wood framed and was on what would later be called Town House Hill overlooking the village. By 1844, there was religious friction in Richford as the Reverend William Miller visited and professed that the end of the

The old Montgomery Methodist church. *Photo by Armand Messier and Northern Vermont Aerial Photography.*

The old Methodist church in Richford. *Photo by Armand Messier and Northern Vermont Aerial Photography.*

world was coming soon. Many people embraced his teachings, and this caused schisms among religious folk.[80] Thankfully, Miller was wrong. A new brick church was built at the falls and was used by the Methodists, Baptists and a group that had recently moved into town, the Seventh-day Adventists. This building was located at the *T* between Main and River Streets, on the east side of the Missisquoi River. This continued until the 1870s, when religious activity expanded greatly. The Adventists and the Baptists had enough of a following and funds to build a church on Main Street. This building also served as the Town Hall. At about the same time, the Methodists built their own new church on River Street. And finally, there were enough Catholics to have their own church, which was built on Liberty Street. The Episcopalians were allowed to use the original old building, on Town Hall Hill.[81] Modern religious structures were built in Richford with the arrival of the twentieth century. In the early 1900s, the old Catholic church was abandoned, and property at the intersection of Troy and Main Streets was used. All Saints Church is the massively impressive brick building in the center of town. About ten years later, the old Union Church building on Main Street, which had housed a number of faiths over the years, was redone as the Town Hall.[82]

Saint Albans, the largest of the Franklin County communities, has the most varied religious history. Many churches have been in different locations over the last two hundred years. The first organized visits were in the late 1790s. Preacher Ebenezer Hibbard came when the population was still only a few hundred and ministered in houses. The Methodists built their church, the first one in town, in 1821. The Congregational Church was built in 1826. Its first minister was the Reverend Worthington Smith. In 1862, the current building was erected. The first Episcopalian church was built in 1825 and was consecrated by Bishop Griswold. St. Luke's Episcopal Church on Bishop Street was erected in the late 1850s and rests on the slope of the hill, overlooking much of the city. The Congregationalists arrived early as well but didn't build. They used people's homes. For a time, they met in the courthouse, but by the late 1860s, they had built a structure on Congress Street.[83] The first Catholics were likely French Canadian priests who moved south after the American Revolution. Their visits were brief stays. There wasn't a substantial Catholic presence in St. Albans until perhaps the 1830s, when the faith became organized in other areas of Vermont. Through the 1840s, '50s and '60s, more Catholics migrated to town, and work commenced on St. Mary's Catholic Church on Fairfield Street. Holy Angels Parish was established in 1872; in 1972, it celebrated

The Catholic church in Richford. *Photo by Armand Messier and Northern Vermont Aerial Photography.*

its one-hundredth year of activity. Catholics were numerous enough on the west side of town that Holy Angels School was created on the property. The twentieth century brought more faiths to the county. The Church of the Nazarene formed in the 1930s. The Northside Baptist Church on Route 7 was built in 1980. Its older sibling is the First Baptist Church, on Congress Street. The origins of the Church of the Rock go back to the 1970s, when a group of locals met for Bible study. As their numbers increased, they associated themselves with the Assemblies of God. In the 1980s, the congregation obtained its current location on Fairfax Road.

In Sheldon, a Congregationalist preacher visited in 1807, but he was just traveling through.[84] The first church was likely Grace Episcopal. It was a wood structure built a decade or two after people moved into town. The Reverend Stephen Beach ministered to a congregation of about forty people. By 1834, there were ninety-two people attending religious services. The Methodists and the Congregationalists shared a building near "The Rock" until 1862. Then, Congregationalists built their own holy building. Attendance went up and then down, until the property was given to the town, which used it as a meetinghouse until it was torn down. The wood building was replaced by a brick structure before the Civil War. Rarely used for religious services, this building still stands. The Methodists, who originally founded "The Rock," continued to use that location until 1859, when the building was renovated. It still stands today. Little is known about the Union Church that once existed in town. Services were offered there between 1860 and 1908, when it was gutted. At one point, there was a Baptist church. In 1906, the United Methodist Church was built. It is on the corner of Route 78 and Rice Hill and is rarely used today.

This material does not cover every church in the county. Nor does it cover all of the history of each faith. Such topics would be worthy of their own books. However, this provides a little context for those beautiful, sometimes mysterious old buildings that anchor our communities.

CHAPTER SIX

LOST RAILWAYS

I n some ways, the stark distinctions between the past and the present are easily seen all over Franklin County yet mostly ignored in daily life. In nearly every town, the history of rail transportation is visible but fading into the past. The remnants live on and have been transformed into other uses, such as the Ron Kilburn Transportation Museum in the former Swanton train depot and the Missisquoi Rail Trail recreation path. People throughout the county enjoy them. Early train travel created Franklin County as it is known today, connecting people economically and socially and leading to rapid development of towns and villages.

Electronic devices and gadgets dominate twenty-first-century existence. The pace of life is much faster than it used to be. Vehicles allow people to work far from home and travel long distances. Planes travel from one side of the continent to the other in half a day.

Imagine a world where none of that existed, where it took months to sail across the Atlantic Ocean and weeks to travel bumpy dirt roads. Life was just slower and more isolated.

Society got a glimpse of the future with the invention of the steam engine in the early 1800s. Used on the nation's internal waterways, steamships allowed rapid and group travel over rivers and lakes. It was so revolutionary that there was a massive investment in the canal system of the Northeast. Products traveled from population centers faster than ever before, economies improved and technological advances increased. If an engine could be used to power a boat in water, why couldn't it do the same over land?

And then came the train.

The first rail line in the United States was just three miles long. It began running in 1826 in Massachusetts, transporting stone to help build the Bunker Hill Monument. Investors, entrepreneurs and engineers excitedly embraced the bulk transport of economic goods. It soon became apparent that large numbers of people could travel conveniently between population centers. The first passenger rail was laid between Charleston and Hamburg, South Carolina, in 1830.

And rail travel took off.

Vermont did not get into the action until the late 1840s. Over eight thousand miles of tracks had been put down connecting the nation's larger cities. Naturally, the first tracks in the Green Mountains were laid in the southern part of the state, being near Boston and New York. By 1849, two lines connected Burlington to the rest of the country. Rail was quickly snaking through the north country.

The first railroad line to be laid in Franklin County was the Vermont and Canada. The main terminus was in Burlington, and by the middle of October 1850, it had reached St. Albans.[85] The tracks were laid through Colchester and Milton and then Georgia into St. Albans. Less than a year later, the northern branch was up to Swanton and Alburgh, connecting Vermont to Upstate New York. This north–south route along Lake Champlain became

The train station in Highgate Springs. *Courtesy of the Highgate Historical Society.*

View of Missisquoi Bay at the mouth of Rock River. The Rock River and I89 bridges are in the distance. All that remains of the train bridge is in the foreground. *Photo by Armand Messier and Northern Vermont Aerial Photography.*

the backbone for future rail throughout Franklin County, with St. Albans being the hub. Then, like vines in the forest, the lines spread to almost every town in the county.

Potential profit was the purpose of any line. If population centers were connected, more money could be made. Until the middle of the 1860s, no line connected Montreal to the East Coast. That was rectified in November 1864. A separate north–south route departed St. Albans and ran through Swanton and Highgate. This line brushed Missisquoi Bay at the mouth of Rock River and went on into St. Armand, Quebec. Travelers and freight were now able to run from Montreal to America's big cities.

With these early lines constructed, others soon followed. By 1870, a smaller east–west connector was under construction, the Lamoille Valley Railroad. While miniscule compared to the larger projects, this line was expansive for the tiny towns of northwest Vermont. From Swanton, it ran due east to Highgate. It connected with the rail recently put down in Sheldon and intersected with the Missisquoi Railroad. Tracks soon connected south Fairfield, small sections of Bakersfield and Fletcher. Eventually, this line linked with rail running through Cambridge.

This page, top: The foundation for this building is on the property where the Swanton Historical Society is located today. *Courtesy of the Swanton Historical Society.*

This page, bottom: The old train bridge over the Missisquoi River in Sheldon. *Photo by Armand Messier and Northern Vermont Aerial Photography.*

Oppostie: A train running through Enosburg. *Courtesy of the Enosburg Historical Society.*

The growth was as explosive as that of a hungry teenager. Just a few years later, St. Albans cemented its status as a terminus for rail east and west. The Missisquoi Railroad, a twenty-eight-mile stretch of track, linked that city to eastern Franklin County along the Canadian border in Richford by 1872. The economic benefits to the towns along the line were immediately felt; suddenly, areas that had been isolated were connected to the rest of the country. This line roughly paralleled the Missisquoi River. It went through the eastern edge of Swanton, ran through the entire length of Sheldon, then northern Enosburg and southern Berkshire and finally into Richford. Richford, situated on the Canadian border, immediately became a hub for freight and passenger travel from Boston and southern New England.

At about the time the Missisquoi connector was worked on, a Canadian company, Southeastern, built a span between the small Quebec village of West Farnham and Richford. A third line out of town was proposed, this one to the east. Business interests wanted to connect northern Vermont to the far reaches of Maine, and research was done to determine if rail could connect Richford and Newport, Vermont. Soon, plans were in development for the Missisquoi & Clyde River Railroad. All of the focus on transportation brought an economic boom to Richford. By 1872, local interests had organized for a bank to be established. The Richford Savings Bank and Trust Company opened in 1875. A tub-making factory, a furniture store, a jeweler, several merchants, a druggist, a dentist and lawyers all set up shop in the community. By 1878, there were two newspapers. Lodging went up to accommodate international travelers. All of this was possible due to the emerging transportation infrastructure. There was even a Wild West–style gun duel in August 1876.[86]

In addition, small trolley lines connected short distances. They were small veins of transport that demonstrated local ingenuity and linked different parts of Swanton and St. Albans. They melded with the availability of transportation dinosaurs—the ferry and the steamship—into a quick and convenient service. The southern portion was a direct link between Saint Albans Bay and the city of St. Albans. Tracks were laid that provided passenger service and hauled freight from the city to the bay. The same situation developed in Maquam Bay, just west of the village of Swanton. Ferryboats docked at a boathouse on the shore, and passengers departed for hotels in town or to visit communities farther to the east. Trolley cars ran from Grand Avenue in Swanton into Saint Albans. Locals and visitors could hop on a San Francisco–like railcar and make quick jaunts north and south.

Sadly, much of this history has been lost.

Prior to rail, the steamships on Lake Champlain did quite well. Rail brought strong competition; steamships are only the subjects of history books now. Rail got its competition in the early 1900s with the invention of the automobile. Rail traffic has been in decline for 150 years. There is only one line running through northern Franklin County today, and it transports goods only. The Central Vermont maintains the tracks that start from Alburgh and enter Franklin County via the bridge over Missisquoi Bay. It runs south through Swanton, within sight of the Swanton Historical Society depot and links with the old mega-hub of rail in the region, Saint Albans. That line still runs south into Chittenden County.

CHAPTER SEVEN

"NORTH OF THE MASON DIXON LINE"

Civil War Nuggets

V ermont is one of the smallest states in the Union. Fighting during the Civil War was much farther south, but the conflict was disruptive to both populations. Many of the battles happened south of Washington, D.C. It was the bloodiest war in American history. In all, seven hundred thousand Americans died during the fight to eliminate slavery. Vermont was far from the fighting, but armed conflict did occur with the St. Albans Raid in 1864. Historical digging exposes many forgotten hubs of Civil War history here. Quite a few locations in Franklin County have become obscured by time.

Vermont often takes pride in having outlawed slavery in 1791. Slavery, however, existed in different forms in the North well into the 1800s. Vermonters were active in the Underground Railroad, the system of safe houses and trails that helped escaped slaves flee the South and find refuge in Canada. Some in Franklin County helped former slaves find freedom. In Georgia, Reverend Alvah Sabin formed the Georgia Anti-Slavery Society in 1836. The group attracted over 110 members, and their meeting place was on Plains Road, about two miles from Route 7. Local lore suggests the brick church there may have been part of the Underground Railroad.[87] Sabin's activities were not limited to the town of Georgia. He became involved with the Anti-Slavery Society and lectured all across the state. In Franklin County, he was quite active. In 1836, he spoke in every single community.[88] He raised over $112 for the National Anti-Slavery Society in New York. Much of this money came from churches in Georgia, Swanton, Franklin and Fairfax.

Many towns have stories of hidden rooms in closets, walled-off hallways or secret chambers in basements where escaped slaves hid from slave catchers. However, most of these stories are likely false. With Vermont's proximity to the Canadian border—literally just a few miles away—it is doubtful that slave catchers ventured so far north. Escaped slaves here would have had little reason to hide. Still, stories about local homes abide.

When the war began, Vermonters answered the call to arms in large numbers. Where these brave men mustered, trained and departed from have their own unique stories, and they are tantalizing pieces of Civil War History.

Perhaps the most interesting story is that of the roots of the Thirteenth Vermont Regiment, part of the famous Vermont Brigade. This unit eventually played the critical role of spoiling Pickett's Charge, the massive Southern infantry attack on the third day of the Battle of Gettysburg. On July 1, 1863, the first day of the battle, Confederates pushed the Union army back through Gettysburg. The next day, there was intense fighting up and down the defensive line. Frustrated, the Southerners launched a massive attack against the Union defenses on July 3. Approximately thirteen thousand Confederate soldiers descended upon the waiting Northerners. The Thirteenth Vermont Regiment was the key unit on the third day of the most critical battle of the war. A textbook flanking maneuver allowed the Yankees to cripple George Pickett's charging rebels.

The Thirteenth Vermont was made up of units from all across the Green Mountains. Two of those companies were mustered in Franklin County. Those men played a defining role in the course of the Civil War.

For this group of Franklin County men, it started when Abraham Lincoln called for recruits on August 4, 1862. Individual Vermont towns organized to recruit enough men to fill the regiment by the middle of August.[89] The unit came together so promptly that most men were not issued uniforms until they arrived at Camp Lincoln, a barracks located in Brattleboro, Vermont.[90]

Company G, from eastern Franklin County, comprised men from Bakersfield, Richford and Enosburg. They mustered in Enosburg before marching to Bakersfield, where they prepared to meet up with the rest of the units.[91]

Company K was assembled from the towns of Franklin, Highgate, Swanton, Grand Isle, North Hero and Alburgh.[92] They gathered in Highgate and drilled in the present-day park at Highgate Falls. Frank Johnson's old hotel on the green was a temporary headquarters.[93] The company, which comprised 126 men, was fully formed and training by September 16, 1862.[94] Their orders came in, and the men were told to board the Central Vermont

Railroad line in Swanton and St. Albans. They did so on the west side of the Missisquoi River, at the end of Depot Street.[95] They departed Franklin County on September 29.[96]

No discussion of Civil War history in Vermont is complete without covering locations associated with the St. Albans Raid. Multiple books and other sources already paint a vivid picture of what happened on October 19, 1864. Confederates traveling to Canada to gain support for their cause robbed three banks in St. Albans, attempted to burn the city and fled before being apprehended north of the border.

There are hidden, lesser-known sites associated with the St. Albans Raid.

The routes the Confederates took into St. Albans involved traveling on the rail lines in Highgate and Swanton. Until the day of the attack, the bandits had originally planned on raiding the Union Bank in Swanton and, possibly, burning much of the town.[97] Those plans changed when the raid began.

They did try to rob another bank during the raid, one that was not in St. Albans. After fleeing the city, they fled to Sheldon and entered the village after 4:00 p.m. The only bank in town, the Missisquoi Bank, had already closed for the night, but the employees were still inside. The raiders pounded on the doors but retreated when they noticed a posse of citizens coming from the south.

This bank in Swanton was almost part of the St. Albans Raid. The building still stands today. *Courtesy of the Swanton Historical Society.*

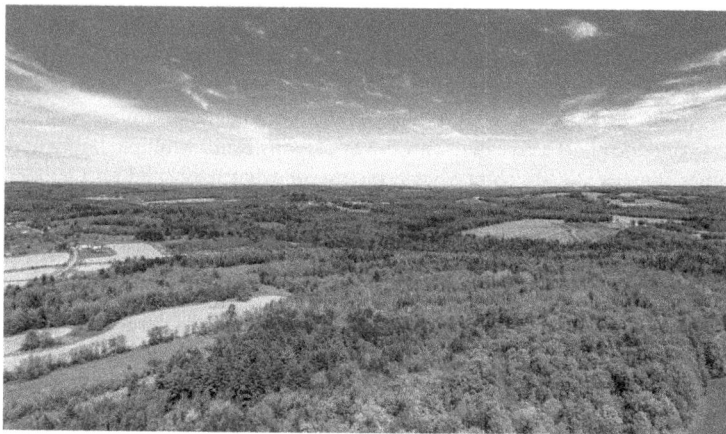

This location in Berkshire is where the St. Albans raiders fled into Canada. *Photo by Armand Messier and Northern Vermont Aerial Photography.*

Their exact escape path is not known; it is believed they continued to travel northeast. At some point, the raiders split. One group went in a northwesterly direction through East Franklin. The second group retreated through parts of Enosburg and then traveled into Canada somewhere near West Berkshire.

Days later, the news became public that the banks had not been the only targets. Stories and rumors spread, some of them true, that the original schemes had been much worse. The hostiles had enough "liquid fire" on them to try to burn St. Albans, but the composition of the flammable substance was likely a bit off. Also, wet weather during the previous few days had left area buildings damp. While the fuel was used in the city multiple times, and again on the bridge covering Black Creek in Sheldon, the damage was minimal. Disrupting the communications system by destroying the telegraph network had been an option. Much later, it was revealed that more ethically dubious attacks had been considered. One involved the spread of smallpox through the local population via infected blankets and clothing. Gangs and bands of rebels were feared to be lurking in Canada, ready to raid again.

It became clear that the events of October 19 might not be an isolated incident, and measures were taken to protect the area. Due to poor relations with Canada, where rebel sympathies ran deep, the governor of Vermont requested federal troops be stationed along the northern frontier.

Following the lead of the armed units that pursued the St. Albans raiders, the rest of the state immediately organized. Groups of soldiers were called to action and sent north. By the night of the raid, soldiers from Camp Lincoln in Brattleboro and others from Montpelier and Burlington were on the train north. They were deployed in the city by the next morning.[98]

Where all of these men patrolled are today's hidden Civil War sites.

As the defense of the northern Vermont border became a pressing need, militia infantry units were mustered into service. Nearly 100 served in St. Albans. Richford called up 60 men under the command of Lyman Smith. Montgomery issued orders to 40. Enosburg had three separate militia units. One group of 39 was stationed along the frontier, 40 were in West Enosburg and another 40 were stationed in Enosburg Falls. In addition, 120 men patrolled in the small community of Berkshire, 60 militiamen served in Sheldon, another 60 were stationed in Swanton and 40 were in Franklin under the command of R.C. Gates. Highgate raised two units of 40 men each under the command of James Holloway.[99] One was for East Highgate and one group for parts north.[100] Some were assigned guard duty at the two bridges over the Missisquoi River. The first was in Highgate Falls, the other in East Highgate.[101] Transportation infrastructure was feared to be a ripe target.[102]

The Vermont State Cavalry was mustered into service as well and sent to the border communities: fifteen horsemen were sent to Franklin,

In the final months of 1864, the Union military patrolled the bridges over the Missisquoi River. *Artwork by Josh Sinz.*

61

twenty-five went to Highgate, thirty worked in Swanton and sixty were in St. Albans. Sheldon received sixty riders, Richford got thirty and Berkshire had another fifteen. These units patrolled into the winter months and remained into 1865.

In St. Albans, the defenders were housed on three separate properties. The cavalry unit spent nights at what today is 225 North Main Street; at the time, it was the Houghton property. Some men were housed at the Silas Hathaway House. As the deployment morphed into a long-term effort, men were at "Camp Holbrook," which was the Horatio Seymour Farm, off Seymour and Sheldon Roads.[103]

There were fears that steamships on the lake would be targets and their crews were armed. Along the coast of Lake Champlain, at the southern tip of Missisquoi Bay in Swanton and Alburgh, soldiers were deployed to protect the long railroad bridge. These men were from Captain Bancroft's company; Sergeant Ward's squad was given the duty of watching the west bank of Hog Island in Swanton over to Alburgh.[104]

The Civil War lasted four years. When the war began, local boys signed up and trained here. In the aftermath of the St. Albans Raid, there was a flurry of action along the border. Vermont is as far away from the South as one could get, but nuggets of Civil War history certainly exist here.

Chapter Eight

Some of Our Early Schools

T he stories of the first schools in Franklin County are pretty obscure. Today, there are union high schools and small area elementary schools. It wasn't always like this.

When the very earliest settlers came, education was much different than it is now. Even into the 1770s, reading and writing was something enjoyed by a lucky few. If families lived near cities and enjoyed a certain social status, education was a possibility. It was much different on the early frontier.

The poor and the middle class had to get by the best they could. Large families were needed to run farms. If parents never received much schooling, their kids might not have had exposure to books. There was just too much work to do. Clearing land and subsistence gardening required backbreaking levels of manual labor. As soon as the kids were old enough to feed the chickens, milk the cows or help in the fields, they did so. Time to read or write was a luxury. The prevalence of religion was a major factor in what was available to read. One of the most available books was the Bible.

It was not until enough people moved to Franklin County that schools emerged; in most cases, they were not large buildings. That concept comes much later, when the populations and tax bases were large enough.

The first schools were usually in people's homes. They had to be. There were no buses and no cars in the early days. Getting to school on horseback was an option for some, but the general practice was that children walked. Grandparents tell stories about struggling in snowdrifts several feet high or walking an hour to get to school. Many of those grumbling grandma and grandpa tales are probably true.

One of the early schoolhouses in Highgate. This one was on St. Armand Road. *Courtesy of the Highgate Historical Society.*

Often in the olden days, education was based on the size of the community. Early on in Bakersfield, the town was divided into two school districts. The town's education history is defined by Bakersfield Academy, established in 1840. For a short time, there were two separate flourishing schools. First, there was the "South Academy"; not long after, the "North Academy" was erected.[105] Many people, including editors from local papers, mistakenly identified one for the other.[106] For a time, the more active of the two was the Bakersfield Academy and Literary Association. In those days, its spring semester did not begin until late February, and the term lasted twelve weeks. In 1845, the trustees advertised that they had obtained an advanced "Chemical and Philosophical Apparatus," and that lecture would be the primary method of study.[107] The students came and went, but the academy tried to appeal to local families. In May 1846, it advertised its summer term and promoted classes in penmanship, French, music, painting and drawing. In addition, the school had added to its offerings with an improved "Astronomical Apparatus."[108] By 1846, 170 students were enrolled. Each term, the school advertised in area newspapers. A decade later, classes in math, civil engineering and ancient languages were offered.[109] By 1859, there was a class in physiology.[110]

Things changed in Bakersfield in 1878, when Peter Bent Brigham, a wealthy individual who'd grown up in the area, donated a large amount of money to the town. He'd become wealthy in real estate, investments and railroads. He gave $30,000 for educational purposes. Improvements were made to the school buildings. The improved Brigham Academy building was impressive—a brick building two stories tall with a hip roof and a central tower that eventually featured a bell.[111] For many decades, Brigham Academy served as a solid venue of higher education. Over time, its focus shifted to being a modern high school. It closed for about two years in the mid-1960s; around 1968, it reopened as the region's middle school. Priorities and locations changed, and in 1986, the Bakersfield Elementary and Middle School opened across the street. The current old building is unoccupied, although the community is having discussions about how to use the historic space.

It is difficult to imagine, but small, one-room schoolhouses populated each town. Franklin County also hosted a few Catholic schools, and for some, religious schools in Swanton and St. Albans were strong pillars in the county.

Different versions of Catholic schools have existed in Swanton since the mid-1800s. They were small and filled the needs of the faithful. One of the first was a tiny building on the southern end of town. In the area of the village, it wasn't until 1896 that parochial education for Catholics was formalized. Substantial renovations to St. Anne's hall brought the high school and the elementary school into the same location, behind where the Church of Nativity now stands. St. Anne's was renovated in 1954 and had eleven classrooms.[112] In 1963, there were 154 high school students and almost 500 in the younger grades.[113] It closed its doors in 1973, ironically at a time when the student population in town increased. St. Anne's students were absorbed into Swanton Elementary. There wasn't enough classroom space, and the community soon came to regret the closing. By 1977, just a few years after the religious school closed, Swanton Elementary classes had to be held in the Swanton Armory. There were so many students that brief discussions were held about reopening St. Anne's. The issue was floated to the public, but community support was lacking. It had closed due to financial reasons, but the church admitted that a lack of younger nuns hampered its ability to deliver religious education.[114]

Another Catholic school was Holy Angels on Lake Street in St. Albans, which was established in 1872. At one time, there were as many as six hundred students enrolled in grades one through eight. Enrollment ebbed and flowed until the school's one-hundredth anniversary. Discussions about its future spilled into the public, when about two hundred children were still enrolled in the elementary grades. The discussion about closing was not related to the number of Catholic families in the area. Holy Angels struggled with the onset of larger public schools, and it further identified two major obstacles. Religious officials publicly blamed the American Civil Liberties Union for its vocal advocacy of the separation of church and state. The Catholic Church also looked inward, and accepted that fewer and fewer local women entering the church was a problem. Young women were not becoming nuns, and this put a burden on the shoulders of older members of the faith.[115] Soon, the Roman Catholic Diocese of Burlington admitted how hard it was to keep the school going. There was a fundraising drive to try to save the school, but there were too many expectations of older nuns. The school was able to hold on for a few more years, but it closed in the mid-1970s.

People can look through old yearbooks to see what schools were like long ago. Historical societies have photos of early school buildings and may have copies of early textbooks, chalkboards and maps. Your local historical society can provide a lot of details on how, when and where your parents and grandparents were educated.

CHAPTER NINE

"BREAKING THE ICE"

Ice Harvesting in Northwestern Vermont

There is a lot of history behind your refrigerator or freezer. Technology can reveal a lot about the past. Today, someone purchases a unit, plugs it in and…welcome to the middle class! Well, what did people do before electricity?

Evidence from archaeological sites around the world reveals that people harvested ice for cooling purposes as early as 3,700 years ago. Typically, only the wealthy had the resources for such an undertaking. Slaves or workers cut huge chunks of ice in winter and transported them to a special structure designed to keep the heat out. Over the months, the ice slowly melted, but the ruling families enjoyed the benefits of having ice available.

Fast-forward a few thousand years—getting individual cooling units into American homes was a reality long before electricity was harnessed. Franklin County has a unique place in this interesting vein of American economic and social history. There was a significant economy around ice harvesting, and Lake Champlain and the Missisquoi River provided locals with the perfect opportunity to deliver a product desired in warmer regions. A lot of manual labor was required, but this area was part of an industry that brought rudimentary refrigeration to middle-class homes and some businesses in the big cities.

The ability to make quality ice depended on the harshness of the season. If winters were not particularly cold, that negatively affected the product. The earliest evidence of harvesting ice for profit appears in an 1875 *St. Albans Messenger*. In a small "community notes" blurb, it was mentioned that

Ice harvesting on the Missisquoi River in Swanton. *Courtesy of the Swanton Historical Society.*

the late January ice crop was better than ever, indicating that the practice had been going on for some time. In some cases, the blocks taken from Lake Champlain were twenty-five inches thick.[116]

There were some mild winters in the late nineteenth century. Local papers reported that the harvest to the south had been poor and companies were searching for quality ice as far north as Lakes George and Champlain.[117] Not surprisingly, the price was high during this period. Local dealers scoured the lakes for the thickest product. In February 1892, John Hunt and M.J. Bascom of St. Albans had three different groups cutting blocks sixteen inches thick. This particular crop filled the village icehouses. Nearly fifty teams dragged ice from the bay to the center of town.[118]

Communities with access to water took advantage. The labor and cost of transportation were less if an entrepreneur had the ability to work the frozen water closer to town. This was the case in Swanton in the early 1900s.[119] Ice was cut from the Missisquoi River and harvested from the Maquam docks on the lake.[120]

Even communities with limited access to rivers got in on the action. Berkshire, which has only a sliver of the Missisquoi River on its eastern border with Richford, took advantage of the local, harvestable resource. In

Ice harvesting in Missisquoi Bay. *Courtesy of the Highgate Historical Society.*

1907, farmers in North Berkshire had trouble dealing with a January thaw. It made the trails in the woods muddy and affected the thickness of the ice.[121] The warm weather didn't affect Joseph Paquette, the local ice dealer from Enosburg. His teams harvested ice one foot thick and filled his two icehouses for the season.[122] Cold temperatures returned long enough for Lake Champlain to freeze, hard. In St. Albans, dealers acquired over five thousand tons. Some of it measured over thirty inches thick.[123]

Even landlocked communities like Fletcher participated. A small portion of the Lamoille River is the southern boundary of the town. Teams were harvesting in January 1908, taking advantage of an extreme cold snap. The temperatures were fifteen degrees below zero. Winter sleighs were used to move the product over the frozen ground.[124] In 1916, farmers in Fletcher harvested ice from Half Moon Pond.[125]

There was work in January 1912 in Sheldon, along the Missisquoi River.[126] Ice was being harvested out of Missisquoi Bay in Highgate Springs in 1914.[127] The winter experienced sustained cold temperatures, and work in St. Albans Bay was done by February 25, and locals had mined enough for the entire season's crop. The product was over thirty inches thick, the best in some years.[128]

Ice harvesting in Missisquoi Bay. *Courtesy of the Highgate Historical Society.*

Advances in technology always bring change. While the harvesters of northwestern Vermont went about getting ice the old-fashioned way—by cutting and using saws—technology brought new competition. By 1912, industrialization and electricity provided "ice factories" and "cold storage warehouses." Large-scale ice and refrigeration units had been developed, particularly near large population centers. Ironically, investors advertised their product as more pure and less likely to have contaminants than that taken from rivers and lakes. The *Messenger* ran an article about the growing competition to local industry in January 1912.[129]

Despite the out-of-state competition, ads ran in local papers letting people know they could enjoy the luxury. Men like N.W. Sanborn harvested "Pure Bay Ice."[130] His ads ran during the cold months of 1913 and 1914. His efforts document the changing industry; in February 1913, he used relatively new technology. He employed a motorized conveyor, which took the ice from the bay to a location where teams of horses or cars transported it.[131]

Prior to the wide use of automobiles, horses did most of the tough work. At times, concerns were raised about the treatment of the teams. Vermont had laws in place to protect animals, but violations still happened. In March 1913, the Humane Society investigated whether local teamsters had forced their horses to move too much weight. Considering the bulk chunks involved, the concerns appear justified. One "cake" of cut ice might weigh as much as three hundred pounds. It was reported that over thirty cakes were in each sleigh, meaning the animals were forced to transport dangerous and unhealthy weights, in some cases over ground that was bare of snow. It was reported that if the activity didn't stop, the Humane Society would contact the state's attorney and push for the enforcement of the laws.[132]

Ice harvesting was not without risk.

In February 1913, locals read about an accident in Richford. A timber support beam fell and landed on Andrew Welch while he was harvesting ice. It struck him across the shoulders, injuring his upper back. He was transported to the St. Albans hospital, where doctors weighed the need to operate on his vertebra.[133] His condition did not improve, and the operation commenced. Doctors told Andrew's family that it would be several days before they knew if he could walk again. Andrew Welch died not long after. An Irish immigrant, he was only forty-five years old. Another, less severe accident happened in February 1919, when B.H. Combs of East Berkshire fell through the ice in the frigid temperatures. He got out of the bone-chilling water and recovered.[134]

The landlocked locations of the county tried to participate in the harvest. While the roads were bad and travel by sleigh was difficult, farmers in Fairfield tried to harvest ice in January 1916.[135]

The business was lucrative enough that, in 1917, a local man constructed an artificial pond. The area is presently one of the most traveled locations in the county, where Interstate 89 curves between Exits 19 and 20. The pond rested in the low area between Aldis and French Hills. A.W. Fisher, who owned a farm in the area, built a dam where several natural springs and small streams flowed. The dam was no small achievement of engineering. When completed, it was 534 feet long and about 9 feet high. Along with the dam, Fisher had an icehouse constructed that measured 180 feet long, 40 feet wide and 22 feet tall. When filled, the structure housed 3,800 tons of ice.[136]

In these days of freezers and refrigerators, and with I-89 directly east of St. Albans, this history is truly hidden.

CHAPTER TEN

SWANTON GETS MORE MILITARY ATTENTION

At about the same time that local ice harvests were going on, the world was on fire. The flames of World War I started in 1914. The great powers of Europe allowed alliances to bring nearly everyone into the "War to End All Wars." For a few years, the United States stayed relatively neutral.

That changed in early 1917, when tensions flared between the United States and Germany. Germany was actively sinking vessels in the Atlantic. The "Zimmerman Note," a communication between Germany and Mexico about the possibility of war with America, brought America off the sidelines. The nation was now involved.

A small piece of military history from World War I played out in Swanton.

With the call to action, Vermont did its part to provide soldiers for the war effort. Fort Ethan Allen in Colchester was used as a training area. By August 1917, thirteen hundred men from the First Vermont Regiment were called up as part of the Twenty-Sixth Infantry Division. They would be deployed to France, but a lot happened before that deployment.[137]

The situation in Franklin County developed quickly, especially for communities near Canada. There was concern that German sabotage teams might hit sensitive targets along the border. The site that drew the most attention was a gun-manufacturing plant located in the center of Swanton. It was a ripe target located so close to the international line. It is the present site of the Missisquoi Valley School District offices, not far from the police station and Precision Tools.

The main grounds where Company B patrolled. *Courtesy of the Swanton Historical Society.*

The supply chain to the military was the concern, and Swanton was a critical cog. The Remington Factory, as it was called at the time, employed over five hundred people. It made cartridges for the army's high-powered rifles. Even as the United States decided to go to war, the wheels were set in motion for a protective detail to be sent to Swanton. Company B of the Vermont National Guard was mustered into service on March 30, 1917, and organized at the St. Albans Armory. The call-up was prompt, and by April 5, every man had his equipment.[138] By April 12, at least twenty-one men from Company B were stationed in town. The military was not taking any risks. As soon as the men arrived, the Town Hall was converted into temporary military housing. Arrangements were made to have some of the men eat at the nearby Riverview Hotel.[139] Some of these volunteers were from St. Albans.[140] The unit's commanders were given the task of increasing recruitment from local, unmarried men. The U.S. government formally asked local papers to not report on the positions of any of the guardsmen or of patrols along the border, citing security reasons.[141]

In wartime, even far away from the fighting, accidents happen. Company B's service was marked by some tragic events. On April 24, Vermont newspapers reported the accidental death of Private Arthur Sweeney. Another soldier's gun accidently discharged, and Sweeney was killed by a bullet going through his chest.[142] Statements by other members of the army suggested that there may have been an incident involving ownership of the rifle. Less than a week later, Corporal Richard Pollard was hit in the leg by a stray bullet from the firing range at the Remington Plant. He was transported in the old Swanton Furniture Store truck to the Saint Albans hospital for treatment.[143]

As the nation geared up for war, the initial deployment was completed. At times, locals were called to serve overseas, and recruitment was required to fill out the ranks. Most of the new recruits were from Swanton and St. Albans.[144] There was another unfortunate incident late in the evening of May 17. One of the guards from Company B was shot near the Missisquoi River. The guard returned fire, but the offender was not captured.[145] As the days slowly grew longer and spring temperatures rose, Company B received a nice public thank-you for its service. The editor of the *Swanton Courier* praised the activities and work of the soldiers.[146] Unfortunate circumstances continued to play out, though. Men were deployed to the town of Richford to guard the bridges. All was going fine on the border, until Mitchell Burnor was struck by a passing train and instantly killed.[147]

The strength and manpower of the company were always in flux. At different times, infantrymen and even commanding officers were transferred to other units. Some were on their way to see combat in Europe. In other cases, a few men were unable to fulfill their commitments, and the National Guard engaged in a significant recruitment campaign to fill the ranks. By July 12, 1917, the ranks were full and many more Franklin County men had signed up.[148] Recruitment efforts remained active during the summer.

In spite of a rough first few months, Company B was able to fulfill its duties along the border. It patrolled rail lines, performed guard duty at the Remington Plant and at other sensitive locations and kept a watchful eye on the roads and bridges leading to Canada. The war was an ocean away, and no incidents of sabotage occurred.

However, while they carried out their duties, the accidents in Swanton didn't stop.

The next year, on the evening of March 28, the International Explosives plant, located on the west side of the Missisquoi River, exploded. It was part of the war machine and received attention from Company B while it was on patrol in Swanton. Two young women, Dora Savage and Nellie Hemingway, were killed. A good amount of the workforce was female, and their employment was an important part of supporting the war effort. The plant had been making primers for the military.[149]

The story of Company B isn't complete without mentioning the honorable career of Corporal Leonard Lord, who enlisted when the United States entered the war. Lord served in Swanton and the surrounding areas as part of his Company B duties. He further answered the call by enlisting in the U.S. Army, serving in the 103rd Machine Gun Battalion. He was killed in the trenches of France on April 12, 1918. One hundred years after his death, Corporal Lord was honored by the Vermont National Guard and members of the community as the first Vermonter who fell in World War I.

CHAPTER ELEVEN

SPANISH FLU IN SMALL-TOWN AMERICA

Today, society is enduring COVID-19.

A little more than one hundred years ago, Vermonters dealt with something similar. Masks, social distancing, constantly washing hands…these are all examples of how life changed as a result of the Spanish flu. The waves of that disease were particularly bad. Public-health alerts are much different now, and general awareness of disease prevention reaches the public much more quickly. In 1918, newspapers were the fastest way to get information to the public. Imagine life without today's technology. No up-to-the minute health alerts about COVID cases. In the previous century, that lack of knowledge permitted an aggressive spread of a pandemic.

The first recorded instance of the Spanish flu was in March 1918. In the United States, it was an army cook in Kansas. He was on a base with about fifty thousand soldiers. By the end of the month, over one thousand troops were hospitalized and thirty-eight persons had died. Different stages of the disease followed and infected five hundred million people worldwide. Exact totals are only estimates, but between twenty million and fifty million people perished. A large factor in the spread of the disease was the deployment of American soldiers to fight in World War I.[150]

In the United States, there were two waves of the disease. The first was during April and May; it wasn't harmless, but it was nothing compared to the brutal second wave. When it hit, local communities had plenty to deal with through October and November.

The closest substantial military installation was in Fort Devens, Massachusetts. Trains carried troops to Fort Devens before they were sent overseas. The soldiers, in many cases not knowing they were sick, interacted with common travelers. Soon, random people brought the flu through Vermont's transportation infrastructure: Rutland, White River Junction, Burlington and St. Johnsbury.[151]

And St. Albans.

Symptoms ranged from fatigue, coughs, strong fevers and nasal hemorrhaging to the most serious reactions, which paralleled pneumonia. In many cases, victims drowned in their own fluid-filled, infected lungs.[152] These conditions first emerged in late September. The *Messenger* gave the virus front-page exposure, rare for the times, considering that most local news was relegated to the inside pages. The largest community in Franklin County, St. Albans, was a mini-epicenter, with 528 reported cases. Many more were suspected. Schools were canceled. Poolrooms closed. Public gatherings were shunned. Even with these public-safety measures in place, the damage had already been done. Entire families were infected. So many calls went out to local doctors that it was impossible for them to see all of the patients. Two doctors and several nurses at the hospital contracted the disease.[153] Deaths were being reported in St. Albans by October 2. It was being discovered that people died quickly from the new threat—in some cases, not long after the first symptoms were detected. As the number of reported cases became a public-health concern, people realized how contagious it was.

The same day, people were reportedly ill and confined to their homes in Swanton. Clothing that had been donated to the Red Cross for Belgian refugees affected by World War I might have been exposed to the disease. The acceptance of donations was temporarily halted.[154]

A week later, the area had well over seven hundred reported cases, with seventeen confirmed deaths, ten in the last three days. There was a suspected flu death in Sheldon, but nobody knew how many people were sick in the county's smaller communities.[155]

By October 11, facts reported by the *Saint Albans Messenger* were gruesome. Families had received news of the death of loved ones from other parts of the country, and more locals were succumbing. Deaths were noted in several towns, including Sydney L. Osborn, twenty-eight, of Fairfield; and Paul Bickford and George Hemingway of St. Albans. There were the deaths of two young boys in St. Albans. Montgomery suffered a possible flu-related death. Clark Merritt died in Sheldon. Several people were ill in Highgate.[156] Schools closed in Highgate and Bakersfield.

A few days later, the situation in St. Albans hadn't gotten better. Some people were falling ill and recovering, but several blocks and street corners experienced outbreaks. People were sick on Federal, Congress, Russell and South Main Streets.[157] Public meetings were canceled in the city. Deaths were reported on Pearl, Lake and Spruce Streets. Others died on Lincoln Avenue and in St. Albans Bay. Local drugstores ran ads for products thought to help fight the illness. There were sixteen patients with flu-like symptoms at St. Luke's Parish House; they were tended to by volunteers and the Red Cross. The virus had snaked through the county, and smaller towns felt the effects. A public appeal went out to the people of Richford, where two people fell ill on October 14, to donate food to those in need. The same day, there was another reported death in Swanton.[158]

There appeared to be a little hope by October 19, nearly three weeks into the crisis. Fewer cases were being reported, but a lot of people were still sick in the city. Nearly everything was locked down. All St. Albans schools, poolrooms, theaters and public gatherings remained closed. They would temporarily stay that way to stop the spread of the virus. Still, fifteen new cases had been reported in the span of a week. Most of them were from households where someone was already infected.[159] The ill were having a tough time of it. By October 21, there were more than half a dozen deaths just in St. Albans, all linked to pneumonia-type symptoms.[160]

Through the rest of October, the worst seemed to have passed, but the area was still feeling the effects. There were deaths in Richford and several more in St. Albans. In Highgate, the two-year-old son of the Sharrow family died. There were several more confirmed cases in Swanton. Franklin had families falling ill, and there was a death in Fletcher. By the end of the month, the situation seemed to at least be under control. The worst was behind the county, but the disease was still picking off citizens here and there.

November opened with the funeral for a St. Albans resident who had died as a result of the virus, but the stay-at-home order was lifted by November 5. Citizens were still urged to be cautious, and schools were allowed to go back into session.[161] The public was reminded to avoid those were who coughing and sneezing. People were asked to not spit in public. In Swanton, the stay-at-home order continued until Sunday, November 10, when churches were allowed to reopen and movie theaters could again take customers.[162] In the third week of the month, the flu was still prevalent, killing a St. Albans man. In Richford, a grade school teacher who had been infected for several weeks returned to school.[163] Enosburg had gone into quarantine when the crisis hit, then lifted it, only to have a resurgence of cases. The town locked down again until November 23, and schools opened the following week.[164]

The county watched its numbers drop despite nearby communities experiencing dangerous upticks in infections. Several people at UVM became ill, and the town of Morrisville had to go into lockdown again. Life slowly got back to normal, but more infections popped up on Grand Avenue in Swanton in the middle of December.[165] Just south of Franklin County, the town of Milton announced that it was completely shutting down again until the first week of January. Fairfield reported more cases. Several citizens in Berkshire came down with the influenza in the last weeks of December.[166] During Christmas and New Year's, there was a flare-up of at least ten cases in St. Albans.[167] On the final day of the month, there were still deaths in Fairfield and Georgia.[168]

The numbers continued to decline into January 1919, and the state began to take stock of what had just happened. At the time, the carnage was not so hidden. When it was all over, 2,146 Vermonters had perished, almost one-third of all deaths counted in the state during 1918 and 1919.[169]

Some historical information is recorded and rarely gets used. Other knowledge is added to archives and brought to the public's attention when needed. With the COVID-19 situation still unfolding, historical data points about past pandemics are critically valuable. This information about how society grappled with a pandemic one hundred years ago is too valuable to remain hidden.

CHAPTER TWELVE

"AND THE RAINS CAME"

The Flood of 1927

Every so often, the weather delivers a "one-hundred-year event."
They happen once every few generations. They are measured
against other massive events that wreaked havoc and destruction.
Our infrastructure was built on the likelihood that severe weather events
don't happen often. The size of a culvert, for example, is calculated to
accommodate certain levels of rain. If water levels surge during wet seasons,
it makes sense for society to invest in bigger culverts, maybe an engineering
study to estimate where overflow might travel. Taxation levels and local
government spending are based on the past. Elected officials listen to
engineers as they calculate risk.

Today's big weather events are measured against the 1927 flood.

When government officials and engineers calculate how bad future
natural disasters might be, they read what happened one hundred years
ago for a worst-case scenario. Another "one-hundred-year event" like the
Flood of 1927 would be a disaster for Vermonters. The population of
the county is much greater. More people live next to the lake and rivers.
Residents are proudly aware of the beauty of the waterways, but they
should also be aware of history.

Thankfully, weather extremes are not like clockwork. For any given
November, the average rainfall is about 3.33 inches. The totals in 1927 were
a little different. The storms of November 2–4 delivered over 5.0 inches of
precipitation. Regions received the average amount for the month in a little
more than two days. There were downpours nonstop, day and night.

It is no mystery where that much water goes. Precipitation falls. If there is too much of it, it fills streams and rivers to dangerous levels. Water rambles over rocks. Brooks surge. Eastern Franklin County rests along the slope of the Green Mountains, which naturally forces water downhill, toward Lake Champlain. So, when communities like Montgomery, Enosburg and Richford flooded, the water had only one place to go: down and east. Towns like Highgate and Swanton experienced the carnage that started upriver. Parts of St. Albans were described as a miniature lake, and countless residents reported cellars full of water. Even the streets of the county's largest community, resting along a hillside, suffered from the wake of the storm. After days of rain, sections of Lake Street in St. Albans were underwater.[170]

Newspapers across the state ran headlines that described the toll of the destruction. There was plenty to report on.

First, existing technology and infrastructure weren't designed for the scale of the event. There was so much water that St. Albans and the surrounding area lost phone contact with the rest of the state. Somehow, the phone lines in Enosburg remained active, but most towns had no contact with the outside world.

Along the Missisquoi River in Sheldon, the Spooner family was forced to move to the second story of their home when water rushed in and rose above the piano. Farmers reported that cattle, pigs and poultry had been swept away by raging waters. The pulp mill located on the river was virtually swept away.[171]

It wasn't just the Missisquoi. In Georgia, the surging Lamoille River ripped the covered bridge from its supports and carried it away. In Swanton, the area of John's Bridge in the southeast portion of town was underwater.

Nearly all rail traffic in the state was brought to a standstill. The trains in Richford were down, and all lines running north–south through St. Albans, Swanton and Highgate were in danger of being canceled.[172] With the washout conditions, engineers feared the fill under the tracks was too saturated and that the ground might give out anywhere along the line.

In Richford, the situation was particularly bad. The entire village had been isolated, with the banks of the Missisquoi overflowing early in the event. Telephone and telegraph communication was down. Residents along the edges of the river saw their property destroyed. Roads exiting the village had either washed out or were underwater. Farmers all along the river reported livestock being washed away; animals that could be saved were being moved to higher ground.[173]

The Flood of 1927 hit eastern Franklin County particularly hard. *Courtesy of the Enosburg Historical Society.*

Enosburg was in bad shape. Nearly everyone in the village joined rescue crews looking for isolated families. Many boats had been deployed as the water was so high it was the only way for rescuers to travel. In one location, a family reported that four hundred hens were gone. Near the river, the icehouse was in danger of floating away. Another farm reported that the water had risen so quickly that the residents had been unable to get their cows out of the barn. The animals were still in place, and the water was nearly over their backs. The Missisquoi was measured to be thirteen feet higher than normal.[174]

Reports from parts of Sheldon continued to be equally dire. Almost all of the residents of North Sheldon had been evacuated from their flooded homes. As in Enosburg, boats were used in many cases. All of the farm fields along the Missisquoi River were underwater. The raging waters had flowed unrestricted over the flat land there, causing barns and farmhouses to flood. Rumors spread that nearly every highway and rail bridge east of town were gone. The swelling Missisquoi River was full of debris. The water was so high in certain areas that rooftops could no longer be seen.

It was impossible to truly assess the effects of the storms until a little time had passed. By November 5, when the water levels across the county finally started receding, people were able to measure the devastation.

The Missisquoi River was well over its banks in Enosburg. *Courtesy of the Enosburg Historical Society.*

Swanton was without power. At least one house caught fire, it was feared because of electrical problems. Travel conditions were so bad that little information was coming in from Richford and Enosburg. There continued to be problems with the phone and telegraph lines. A local National Guard platoon of thirty-five men was activated. They helped out with the power situation in St. Albans and patrolled the business district to prevent looting.[175]

A dangerous situation developed in East Berkshire. The East Berkshire bridge over the Missisquoi River still stood, but it threatened to give way at any moment. It wasn't only the raging waters that caused problems. Nearly one thousand feet of trees, board debris and storm runoff clogged a slight bend in the river.

In Richford, a different situation developed. The bridge over the Missisquoi River was still there, but the road on either side had been swept away. Shattered chunks of fill added to the situation downriver in Berkshire. Additionally, the Canadian Pacific Railway Bridge was deemed too dangerous to travel across. An eight-foot span of trestle was damaged. At least ten Richford businesses reported major damage. The Richford telephone office had been swept away. The only reports getting to the local paper were through the telephone repair crews in Enosburg.[176] As the crisis

The area of John's Bridge in Swanton was underwater. *Courtesy of the Swanton Historical Society.*

ebbed, Swanton still experienced power problems. It was discovered that John's Bridge, the main route connecting Swanton and St. Albans south of the village, was severely damaged. In Highgate, the bridge over the Missisquoi River was still intact, but a dangerous situation developed when an entire barn was witnessed floating down toward the dam. Several businesses near the river had been damaged.[177]

Conditions in Enosburg were not much better. The East Enosburg highway bridge had been carried away from its supports. It had become part of a jam about forty yards from the concrete bridge in Enosburg Falls, but at least the rest of the bridges in that area still existed. Each was deemed unsafe for any travel. Houses and business had been swept away. Near the border with East Berkshire, in the Black River Valley, farms were gone. Several farmers listed dozens of cows missing, just swept away. One farmer reported having lost one hundred cattle. Another lost all of his cows and pigs and four horses.[178]

In Fairfax, just up the hill from St. Albans, the power was out. The Fairfax Public Electric Light Company was finally able to evaluate the damage to its facility after the water finally receded. In Sheldon, in the area of Shawville, the bridge by the pulp mill had washed away.

After a few days passed, the waters receded, and people took full stock of the enormity of the catastrophe. By November 7, water had gone down enough to allow regular bus traffic, at least over undamaged roads. Travel was finally possible between St. Albans and Richford. However, near Richford, people had to depart the bus, carefully walk over what remained of Nutting Bridge and get on another bus on the east side of the river. Power was restored in most parts of the county, but that was little comfort to those directly impacted. Fourteen people were homeless in the village of Enosburg, another twenty-five in the north part of town.

Even the small community of Franklin suffered—and no portion of the Missisquoi River flows through town. The problems occurred in South Franklin, where there was enough cascading water to sweep sixty cows away. Several barns were damaged.[179]

Of all the affected areas, Richford had been hit the worst. Early estimates had property damages at over $1 million. An entire house from East Richford had been swept away by the angry waters of the Missisquoi, traveled into the village and impacted the bridge on Main Street. It hit with such force that the span was taken out. The house and bridge were pushed farther into town, ripping away the sides of buildings. There was so much water in the village that a channel four feet deep formed on River Street. Several homes were gutted. Roads and sidewalks had been torn up by the water pressure.

The damage in Montgomery Center was significant, even days after the rains stopped. Those surveying the aftermath needed to exit their cars and maneuver around debris.[180]

A countywide boil water order was issued. The Red Cross helped manage a large survey of the area. Their relief effort involved twelve teams traveling to every corner of the county with packets of typhoid serum, for use by those who had contaminated drinking water.[181]

The federal government became involved in the relief effort, and Secretary of Commerce Herbert Hoover toured the state. The cleanup was hindered by the wet weather that continued into December of that year. The persistent rainstorms caused further flooding more than a month later. This was a solemn reminder of how bad things had been: the Flood of 1927 killed eighty-four Vermonters, including the lieutenant governor.

Almost a century later, the story of the Flood of 1927 is hidden away in history books and little-read newspapers. Historical societies have a few images. It is difficult to imagine all of that water and the damage it caused.

One wonders about the next one-hundred-year event…and when it could happen.

CHAPTER THIRTEEN

"TAKE ME TO THE MOVIES"

A New Form of Entertainment Comes to Town

Entertainment technology has changed rapidly in the last one hundred years; few industries have experienced such a rapid metamorphosis. Before the late twentieth century, live performances were the norm. Early devices allowed people to listen to limited offerings. Eventually, early films were shown in small local theaters.

It's so different today. Families don't have to leave their homes to find the entertainment they desire. *Star Wars*? It's on Disney Plus. *Star Trek*? It's on Paramount Plus. *Game of Thrones*? HBO. All of those episodes of *Cheers* are on Netflix. It seems like every movie ever made is on some streaming service. Families once had to huddle around old radios or black-and-white televisions. Now, some living room flatscreens are larger than those used by small, artsy theaters.

Today, there is just one movie theater in Franklin County, the Weldon Theatre in St. Albans. When people don't have the time or desire to drive to Burlington for stadium seating or advanced stereo sound systems, they stay local and enjoy our screens.

The tale of the county's first movie venues is as old as the technology itself.

When the early film industry developed in the late 1800s, venues were used by companies who traveled to towns, bringing projection technologies to rural areas. Larger cities got more options; smaller towns, not so much. Communities needed event halls to accommodate the projectors and enough space for a crowd. Area newspapers ran stories about the new entertainment for months. The earliest date the term *moving picture* appeared in local papers was in March and April 1897. The Opera House in St. Albans hosted a "vitascope exhibition."[182] That same machine was probably used in Enosburg's "Opera Hall" on May 14. Even the paper's wording seemed awkward, unsure of how to describe the new experience. Folks were encouraged to view the "celebrated electrical moving pictures produced by the vitascope."[183] There was quite the public discussion, including if watching constituted immoral behavior.

There were more companies in the area, and more shows in St. Albans. The local paper embraced it.[184] In Swanton, there were as many as four locations where early moving pictures played. One was "Bullard's Hall," which hosted the moving pictures in early September 1897. The *Swanton Courier* noted that the event was not well attended and implied that the public was not giving the newest entertainment a chance.[185]

By the turn of the century, more venues sought to bring movies to the public. In St. Albans, Waugh's Opera House ran substantial ads in local papers glamorizing the experience. These were not the small ads of three years earlier. The moving pictures had become an event of their own, worthy of significant ink. With the arrival of the twentieth century, the technology became more prevalent in the area. Such occurrences were the talk of the city. Small-town Vermont got its fair share of opportunities to witness the craze spreading across the nation.

In March 1900, Paine's Moving Picture Company visited Sheldon.[186] A church in Swanton hosted Passion Play Moving Pictures, displaying its Kinetoscope Machine and showing its most recent production.[187] In October 1901, Laing Brothers was in East Fairfield at Read's Hall with its moving picture machine.[188] About a month later, East Enosburg hosted J.M. Foss and Sons at the schoolhouse. The event was well attended.[189] By 1903, there were shows in Richford and West Enosburg. More shows were advertised and scheduled in East Fairfield, East Berkshire and Swanton in 1905.

In those early years, Swanton developed quite the relationship with the technology. One property in Merchants Row hosted them. The movies were shown at the old town hall. As one decade ended and another began, seasonal movie theaters emerged. In 1910, the town hosted a small movie theater, the Past Time. It was located where the library parking lot is today.

The emergence of single sites devoted entirely to showing films was a watershed for the industry. The public was showing interest in viewing movies on a regular basis. The small traveling movie companies had begun to die out. In St. Albans, the Waugh Opera House was now regularly hosting

One of the area's first movie theaters, the Past Time in Swanton. *Courtesy of the Swanton Historical Society.*

films.[190] Another venue in the city was called the Theatorium. In Enosburg, an early version of a movie theater was the Ayer Opera Hall.[191]

St. Albans had more movie theaters than one might think. Starting in 1911, it had the Bellevue Theatre in the center of town. It was located where Subway recently did business, and the aura of the theater still exits with the classic full-windowed doorframe. For a short time, there was the Empire Theatre, which opened around 1913. It showed films for a five-cent fee.

Other locations tried to use films to anchor their business, like the Dreamland Theater and Bullard's Hall in Swanton. Both the Pastime and the Dreamland theaters operated for almost a decade, until 1917, when a fire gutted the Pastime. At about the same time, the owners of Bullard's Hall opted to create a state-of-the-art movie theater, one that would be the envy of moviegoers throughout the county.[192] What was shown were not even movies by today's definition; quite often, they were clips or scenes sometimes accompanied by a live pianist. By 1915, Richford had the Colonial Theater.

In the 1920s, most of the event hall venues were no longer used for films, although the Sheldon Town Hall was still used occasionally. The industry had changed, and most film entertainment required a true movie theater. By 1924, the Enosburg Playhouse was in full operation and advertising with other area theaters.[193] The Empire Theater in St. Albans was still operating

Left: An advertisement for films at the Enosburg Playhouse in the 1950s. *Courtesy of Theresa Benoît Carman.*

Below: Enosburg schoolchildren enjoying a show at their hometown movie theater. *Courtesy of the Enosburg Historical Society.*

YOUR FAMILY THEATRE
RICHFORD
Drive-In Theatre
RICHFORD. VT.– ROUTE 105 – PHONE NO. 401
ADMISSION ADULTS 50¢
CHILDREN UNDER 12 IN CARS FREE
SHOW STARTS AT DUSK
CARTOON BEFORE EVERY SHOW
MOVIES UNDER THE STARS!
SUNDAY–MONDAY MAY 23–24
THE TERRIFIC LOVE STORY OF THE LOST TRADER WHO BECAME A SOUTH SEA RULER!
BURT LANCASTER
"His Majesty O'Keefe"
FILMED IN THE FIJI ISLANDS!
JOAN RICE
ANDRE MORELL
TECHNICOLOR
PLUS!
THRILLS that Hit Like a .45 Slug!
CHINA VENTURE
starring
EDMOND O'BRIEN
BARRY SULLIVAN
JOCELYN BRANDO

Opposite: Richford had a drive-in! *Courtesy of Theresa Benoit Carman.*

Above: The St. Albans Drive-In will be missed. *Courtesy of Diane Mock.*

when the Weldon came to town around the early 1940s. During the Roaring Twenties and the Great Depression, the modern-day movie theaters developed and thrived.

Enosburg had one, which operated independently of the Opera House. It was just down the street. Richford had a drive-in theater for a short time. It was strategically placed west of town on 105, across the road from the present Border Patrol building.

A few years ago the area lost its only remaining drive-in. It was in St. Albans, and countless adults remember warm evenings with that large outdoor screen. They can recall the small parking ridges in the field. The smell of greasy fries and melting cheese came from the pistachio-green concessions building. Kids waited on the small playground for films to begin. Children fell asleep in back seats. First dates happened. Family photo albums probably have memories captured there. The big outdoor screen always had a few panels missing in spring, and it was always repaired for the summer season. The venue wasn't extravagant, and near the end, it wasn't particularly well taken care of. For those too young to remember, it was located near Interstate 89's Exit 20. It's another example of what has been lost.

The county's only remaining theater is the Weldon, in the heart of downtown St. Albans.

CHAPTER FOURTEEN

"CAN'T I JUST HAVE A DRINK?"

Prohibition in Franklin County

Alcohol is one of the most hidden topics in Vermont history. For decades, the state flirted with being dry. This was even before the prohibition efforts of the twentieth century. Anyone who wanted alcohol needed to avoid attention. Drinking was kept out of the public eye. State and community efforts to control consumption created a patchwork of rules and regulations that set the stage for the 1920s.

Vermont's decision to embrace the prohibition of alcohol came from the values of the Progressive Era, when people had faith that government could be a force for good in people's lives. Most agreed that regulating railroads, cleaning up the meatpacking industry, breaking up monopolies and giving women the right to vote were fine accomplishments.

Outlawing alcohol? The jury is still out on that one. The effort has been collectively defined as government overreach. So many people kept drinking that the government struck the prohibition language from the Constitution a little more than a decade after it was passed.

But the Roaring Twenties was a thirsty era.

The federal government tried to reject alcohol and all of the problems that went with it by 1920. In an era filled with the fervor of reform, people believed in the overall goals of the Eighteenth Amendment. Eliminating alcohol would improve many societal ills. Passing the initiative was one thing; enforcing it was something else entirely.

The challenges for law enforcement in Vermont began with the state's proximity to three large cities in the Northeast—Boston, Montreal and New York. Canada wasn't dry; the product the United States had made illegal was abundant just north of the border. Organized crime came to see the border as a line that simply needed to be crossed.

What made the situation worse was the confluence of ways people could get over the border. Automobile traffic rumbled over the back roads of Franklin County, many of them with no checkpoints. The trainlines went through the northwest shoulder of the state, connecting points north and south, east and west. Vermont's position along Lake Champlain meant that contraband was going to show up in boats. So, not only was prohibition a concept people had to buy into, but the government also had to enforce it on rail, over roads and farm fields and on the waters of the broad lake. History shows that it was an almost impossible task.

As early as 1919, when the nation was still mulling over whether to take the giant leap to prohibition, the government decided it needed an increased presence along the Canadian border. Swanton received more border agents, tasked with the specific duty of seeing that beer, wine and liquor stayed north of the forty-fifth parallel.[194] Several months before the entire country defined itself as a dry nation, border agents were making seizures. In an incident in August, four gallons of liquor were seized from a car believed to have originated in Phillipsburg or Pigeon Hill, Quebec. It had been traveling south into Highgate Springs.[195] In October, a Swanton man was detained twice in one day for trying to bring booze over the border, each time in different cars.[196] It was a preview of things to come.

By December 1919, there was a serious uptick in amounts being seized. On December 15, papers reported that smugglers had gotten their product as far south as Swanton and two locals were taking it to St. Albans. They were stopped on the electric car between the two towns and had four gallons of "high wines" with them.[197] Just before Christmas, a man with twenty-eight quarts of Canadian whisky was arrested.[198] Finally, during the peak of the holiday season, men from Highgate were discovered hiding ten twenty-gallon kegs of whiskey in their hay barn.[199] Vermont had voted to make alcohol illegal, but the Eighteenth Amendment was not even the law of the land yet. Questions began to crop up for law enforcement. How much was getting through? What was hidden away, undetectable?

A lot.

The initiative was unenforceable in any meaningful way. Perhaps it could have succeeded if every local resident embraced it, but that was not going to happen. Some people understood the economic reality well. With alcohol illegal, its supply would be reduced. With supply restricted, the price would go up.

With Franklin County's old backwoods dirt roads, almost anyone could test the new laws. If there were only five main roads that connected each border town with Canada, then there were at least twenty obscure routes by which contraband could flow over the border. The customs house set up in Swanton didn't have enough staffing or automobiles.

The northern edges of Highgate, Franklin, Berkshire and Richford quickly became a no-man's-land of illegal trade. Some of the state's newspapers reached out to Canadian officials. Although U.S. customs officers were seizing what they could, Canadian officials speculated that the law was violated hundreds of times each day.[200]

Border agents began to find cars with hidden compartments in them. Whispers spread that rumrunners were already using the lake. Up in the northwestern corner of the county, Missisquoi Bay was fairly isolated. The railroad bridge between Swanton and Alburgh was a physical impediment to all but the smallest watercraft, allowing stealthy small boats in and out of the bay. What officials could never get a grip on was the possibility that small boat traffic ran between resort establishments and camps. Canoes, fishing vessels and small motorboats had easy access to any dock between the Canadian towns of Phillipsburg and Clarenceville, Quebec. Speed benefited anyone transporting alcohol over the water. If a border agent waited on shore, or if a customs boat searched the bay, loads could easily be dumped overboard. There is plenty of local speculation that if anyone searched the lake floor near Highgate, a few one-hundred-year-old contraband bottles might be found.

On land, the size of the seizures increased exponentially. In the first months, bottles and kegs had been seized. Soon, agents found amounts impossible to easily conceal. Suspicion mounted that smugglers loaded up multiple vehicles to the max and just sent them south at the same time, knowing most would get through. By October 1920, customs agents no longer found quarts or bottles. Dozens of cases were found in vehicles.[201]

Left unanswered is the extent that the tentacles of organized crime were involved in the rum-running. Early clampdown efforts nabbed many locals and some out-of-state traffickers. However, the amounts grew at an alarming rate. Out-of-state vehicles were stopped, chock-full, and officials came to the conclusion they were destined for points much farther south. Suspicion mounted that organized crime was in the area, feeding Boston and New

York. To make the point, in November 1921, a man from New York City had 146 quarts of champagne and whiskey in his vehicle.[202] How many others got through?

Local establishments got in on the action, understanding that there was money to be made if they could serve those who "just needed a drink." Two locations were notorious for these activities: the Highgate Manor and Queen Lil's in Richford. Local lore includes stories of parties, flappers, jazz music and plenty of illegal activity. One legend that stretches the truth is that notorious crime boss Al Capone stayed at the Highgate Manor. While this may be true, there is plenty of evidence to suggest that Capone didn't need to come to the Canadian border to monitor shipments. He had a lot of money and could have paid any of his henchmen for the task. Still, local stories like this can sometimes be true.

The government knew there were increased and intensified enforcement. St. Albans was named the headquarters for prohibition on Lake Champlain. This was initiated in July 1924. The first craft devoted to lake patrol arrived in Burlington by rail and was launched from that city. It motored to the docks being upgraded in St. Albans Bay. The ship was twenty-six feet long and could achieve speeds of forty-five miles per hour.[203]

Despite this increased push on multiple fronts, booze was still coming south in shocking numbers. In July, border agents inspected the train cars coming through Franklin County from Canada. They discovered approximately twenty-two thousand bottles of beer stuffed into a freight car that was supposed to be hauling lumber. The smugglers were now using every method of travel to get contraband by border agents.[204]

The first big seizure for the boat patrol happened in June 1925, when twelve hundred bottles of beer were secured in a scow off Plattsburgh.[205] Not long after, a customs boat stationed in St. Albans stopped men in a canoe off the coast of Isle la Motte. The men had about seventy quarts with them and were headed for Cumberland Head, just north of Plattsburgh. They admitted delivering from Canada and said they would have been paid nicely.[206] In August, a customs patrol boat from St. Albans operated near the bridge in South Hero. After dark, they reported two suspicious vehicles out and about. Border agents on land seized the first vehicle, a King sedan, which had twenty cases of hooch in it. The second, a Cadillac, attempted to drive back up the islands toward Canada but was intercepted in Alburgh.[207] Thirty cases were taken from that vehicle.

By the middle of the 1920s, with Prohibition in full effect, cracks formed in the government's effort to try to persuade people to live better lives.

The Highgate Manor in the early twentieth century. Local lore suggests that a lot of illegal alcohol was consumed here. *Courtesy of the Highgate Historical Society.*

In the spring of 1925, Geraldine Farrar, a nationally known performer, traveled by train through the area. She had made some of the earliest radio performances, had performed with the New York Metropolitan Opera and had made almost seven hundred appearances nationwide. Her career was so significant that she earned a star on the Hollywood Walk of Fame. She had worked in Montreal and traveled by rail through Rouses Point. Her next performances were in southern Vermont. However, customs officials found contraband in her personal car. It was not an insignificant amount. About forty bottles of good champagne, whiskey and beer were found behind the car's ventilators. Some liquor was in the piano, more in the back of a footboard.[208] Farrar was allowed to proceed to her next performances, leaving local folks wondering about the administration of justice. Plenty of them had been arrested for moving alcohol.

Meanwhile, the men assigned to customs duty on Lake Champlain were trying to do their jobs. A few snapshots highlight how busy and how dangerous the work was.

In August 1927, a seventy-five-foot barge was seized on the lake. Hay and agricultural feed was layered on top of copious amounts of alcohol.[209]

Almost a year later, St. Albans officials stopped a rowboat with 240 quarts of ale destined for points south.[210] One of the more unique busts happened when the men searched five cars parked on the steamboat *Vermont.* They found $50,000 worth of contraband, which far outpriced the value of the automobiles. On the market, the cars would have sold for $15,000.[211]

As the ice departed from the lake in 1929, the first seizure happened in late spring. A yacht near Isle la Motte was nabbed with 480 bottles of ale on board.[212] The 1929 numbers tell how active the customs patrol boats were. By December, they had searched forty boats per month, many of them within miles of the Richelieu River.[213]

The work could be extremely dangerous. In one instance in 1931, an agent from Rouses Point fell off the patrol boat while pursuing smugglers. Three men from Burlington were arrested for reportedly throwing their haul overboard. Afterward, the search for the missing official proved fruitless for several days. Agents and boats from St. Albans were used in the search, as well as flyovers with planes from the airport in Highgate.[214] In 1932, a government boat intercepted a suspicious craft running at high speeds. The craft was stopped, but when agent Lawrence Izard boarded the offending vessel, he was struck on the head with a baseball bat. The life preserver he wore saved his life.[215] Authorities were on the lookout for the man responsible.

Part of the hidden history of the county involves a lot that was not documented. Considering the public record of arrests and seizures, one has to put a lot of validity into stories of "back road smuggling."

Many families have oral histories about great-grandparents who were part of the illegal trade. Some may have had equipment for making alcohol stored in the back of an old cellar.

Younger generations have probably heard about the family member who drove cars full of wine and whiskey through Highgate Richford, Berkshire or Franklin.

There are accounts of farmers being paid to keep massive loads of hooch in their barns.

Many of these accounts are true.

All of this illegal activity ended a few years into the 1930s, when Prohibition was repealed.

A good amount of this activity went undocumented. It had to be hidden.

Now, nearly one hundred years later, historians can only try to put the puzzle pieces together.

CHAPTER FIFTEEN

"A DIFFERENT SOCIAL SAFETY NET"

The Poor Farm

Sometimes, accounts of the past should never be analyzed under a modern lens. History can challenge our values, and it can be inappropriate to apply the ethics of the present to years gone by. One example would be the poor farms. Such institutions reveal much about how small towns dealt with the disadvantaged and the poor.

In early America, dealing with the vulnerable and destitute was based on English law from the 1600s. Towns were obligated to set up a system to aid those in need.[216] Initially, churches were expected to provide aid. Then, local communities added another level of care. As systems developed, towns instituted a poor tax and elected an overseer of the poor.[217] As early as 1797, less than a decade after statehood, a law was passed in Vermont forcing villages to deal with poverty at the local level.[218] New Englanders saw two populations in need of assistance. Those who were able to do labor often were the first target population. It was better to find someone farm chores rather than allow them to remain homeless or start stealing from people. The other group that received attention was those unable to work. Widows, children, the injured, the elderly or people with disabilities or medical conditions often needed help to survive. In an age when small communities had agricultural economies, locals looked to the poor farm as a basic safety net.

Several townships had poor farms. Alburgh had one.[219] Early on, so did Georgia.[220] The biggest one in Franklin County was located in Sheldon and was a joint venture. Swanton, Fairfield, St. Albans and Sheldon put up most of the funding in 1834.[221] However, many nearby communities took

The poor farm in Sheldon. Prior to efforts by the federal government, this was the social safety net for local towns. *Artwork by Josh Sinz.*

advantage of the services. It was established on about 150 acres and located on a poorly maintained road. In the early decades, those who were assigned to the poor farm were referred to as tramps and vagrants. While this might sound a little cold, life was much tougher in the early nineteenth century. Often, families were expected to help out relatives when they could.

Once the Sheldon Poor Farm was established, the people lodged there didn't have an easy go of it. Early regulations established that people were expected to work on the farm. Period. Those who didn't might not get meals. Anyone who created problems could be shipped off to the earliest versions of the state mental institutions.[222] Random accidents struck those unlucky enough to be at the poor farm. In October 1873, Philo Baker was run over by a train on the Missisquoi Railroad, just east of what was then called Green's Corners. Baker was reportedly deaf and had been walking on the tracks. He did not survive.[223]

At this early juncture, Harmon Butler of Sheldon, a Civil War veteran, was the first superintendent.[224] By 1868, the effort had expanded beyond the original four towns. Highgate, Franklin and Enosburgh had actively joined the Sheldon Poor Farm Association. This was part of an effort by towns to keep the expense of helping the poor at a minimum.[225]

In 1874, the Overseer of the Poor for St. Albans requested an increase in his budget of a few hundred dollars. The amount was for much-needed improvements at the Sheldon location. Every little bit of positive press helps, and local news reports on the request for funds was favorable.[226] By 1875, Harvey Barnes ran the effort, and the output of the farm was public information. Record numbers of crops had been raised: 240 bushels of corn, 350 bushels of potatoes and 250 bushels of oats. The farm had cut enough hay for twenty cows.[227]

The larger communities sometimes felt that the tax burden often fell on their shoulders. In 1879, some of these feelings were printed in the *Saint Albans Messenger*. Two of the smaller towns, Highgate and Sheldon, had each sent fourteen individuals. The much larger St. Albans had only sent fourteen people. Residents from the city rightly observed that the tax burden was far from equally distributed. Highgate had contributed $352, Sheldon $270. However, St Albans taxpayers had a bill of $1,140. Some speculated that the city should withdraw its support and relocate its disadvantaged to a smaller location within the town.[228]

Occasionally, people taken in at the Poor Farm ended up dying there. This was the case with Mrs. O'Hear, an elderly woman from St. Albans who passed away on the farm in 1882.[229] A tragic incident occurred in the spring of 1886. A ten-year-old girl was rescued from the poor farm with the expectation that she would be taken in by a local family. Just months later, the youngster was back in the care of local officials after having suffered beatings by the family.[230] The communities tried to give a little extra at times. In December 1888, the King's Daughters from St. Albans put on a performance and brought gifts.[231]

At about this time, there was a policy change at the state level. In 1890, two institutions opened up that alleviated some of the burden on local communities. Waterbury and Brattleboro built facilities to better accommodate the "mentally insane"; afterward, local poor farms were not forced to take on so many high-need individuals.[232]

In 1893, there was a massive fire at the Sheldon Poor Farm that destroyed both of the large barns and a large sum of the supplies. No one knew how the fire started, as smoking was prohibited and lanterns were not allowed in the barns. The disruption to daily life was painful, and the immediate effects hit hard. Forty-one cows were saved, but much of the machinery was lost.[233]

There were certainly ups and downs. In November 1897, the *Saint Albans Messenger* reported on the conditions on the property; many on the board of directors had to defend the institution publicly.[234] The paper went out of its way to detail buildings in need of repair and unsanitary conditions that harmed residents. The board did its best to combat the information by sending in letters to the editor. The *Messenger* wasn't done and once again reported on the grim conditions. The property was described as reeking and filthy, and the new barn constructed after the fire was considered a better living arrangement than some of the residential buildings. At the time, there were sixty-three "paupers" (unemployed or homeless) living there, and the newspaper went to great lengths to convince its readership that all was not right with the venture. The paper claimed that the living quarters were the same units erected fifty years earlier. In winter, there was only one stove to keep everyone warm. The paper partially placed blame on taxpayers, reminding them of their duty to follow the money and expect better. Twenty-eight of the residents were children. Five people had died within the previous year, and the unsanitary conditions might have been why. In one instance, a young mother was living in one room with her six children. Oddly enough, many of the residents claimed that the situation wasn't too bad but expressed a desire for better clothing and food.[235] In 1900, more bad news hit when the state had to be called in to inspect the farm's dairy herd. Twenty-one of the thirty-eight cows were suspected of suffering from tuberculosis. Fifteen of the animals needed to be put down.[236] Another snapshot came from a small Richford newspaper in February 1907. It reported that there were sixty-two "inmates." The previous year, there had been eight deaths.[237]

Random accidents were common. In 1910, James Eccles was injured while lighting a firecracker. Only one finger remained, and his hand ended up being amputated at the wrist.[238]

Fate was not kind. Another fire occurred in January 1913. Forty-four people were housed there at the time. No one was hurt, and none of the animals were injured, but four of the structures were destroyed, including the administrative building and the hospital. The local bucket brigade helped contain the fire and limited the damage.[239] Some residents needed to be taken in by local families for the rest of the winter.

Less than ideal conditions were discovered again in 1927, when Vermont's assistant commissioner of public welfare, a Mr. Corliss, visited. He reported that things were not good on the property.[240] The main office building was rotting and filthy. He found bedbugs in the living areas and noted that the mattresses were needlessly uncomfortable, as they were filled with straw. He removed a young boy; state law prohibited the really young from being there for more than ninety days. In this youngster's case, nobody seemed to have cared that he had been there considerably longer.

It wasn't always a sad state of affairs or a worst-case scenario. In 1902 and 1903, there were outbreaks of smallpox in Sheldon. Cases were confirmed in town; none were reported at the property.[241] In 1907, the institution took in the family of a man who was serving time in jail. A wife and five children were housed throughout the winter, receiving support long enough to hopefully get back on their feet.[242]

The United States has always been evolving. The mindset about how such a prosperous nation treats its disadvantaged citizens changed. While many perceived the poor farms as a noble effort, there was a growing consensus that poverty needed to be tackled at the state and federal levels. The American Red Cross and the Salvation Army formed in the early twentieth century with a focus on helping those in need. When poverty ballooned in the 1930s due to the Great Depression, public works programs were adopted nationwide to put people back to work. America looked inward and redefined unemployment. It reexamined the social safety net and made the conscious choice to better help those who had gone without.

Due to this emphasis on helping the needy, many of the state's poor farms closed down. Local communities were no longer independently tasked with helping the most vulnerable. The Sheldon Poor Farm continued to serve a purpose well into the 1960s, but with the arrival of Lyndon Johnson's Great Society programs, the social safety net went through another paradigm shift. The nation took on responsibilities that local towns had struggled with for over a century.

The Sheldon Poor Farm's last year was 1968.

Chapter Sixteen

"WE ALL SUFFER FROM A DEPRESSION"

Public Works Comes to the Area

T he 1920s and 1930s are probably the best examples of the economy roaring along, crashing and then people and businesses turning to government for a solution.

It was the Depression, and some of its landmarks dominate the county landscape.

The world went to hell in a handbasket on October 29, 1929, when the stock market crashed. Herbert Hoover was president, and the appropriate government response was debated for some time. The Depression widened, and when people became concerned about their savings, many went to the banks to get cash out. Such events revealed problems with debt and the banking system that few understood. When everyone tries to take their cash out at the same time, that is called a bank run. The system does not keep enough money on hand to equal all of the cash in customer accounts. Banks around the nation started to close.

By late 1933, nearly 5,500 banks had gone under, deepening the nation's overall financial crisis.[243] However, as of February 1932, no single bank in Vermont had gone out of business.[244] The poor-performing economy lumbered along for several years, but this region's banks weathered the storm, and it appears none went out of business.

Unemployment was a different issue.

Once Franklin Roosevelt became president, he placed an emphasis on putting people back to work. If the private sector did not have enough capital to create jobs, Roosevelt was convinced that the public sector needed

The St. Albans Bay Park. This was an early Depression-era project. *Photo by Armand Messier and Northern Vermont Aerial Photography.*

to try. Several national bills worked their way through Congress, and public works projects were developed locally to help people earn a paycheck.

One of the most visible is the Missisquoi Bay Bridge connecting Swanton and Alburgh. For generations, ferries were the main method of transport over the relatively shallow waters of Missisquoi Bay. Then rail extended into the region. There were a few small floating barges that carried people east and west just north of Maquam Bay. The Depression hit, and road transport over the lake was deemed a worthy project.

In 1934, two years into Roosevelt's first term, there were discussions about public and private partnerships that could deliver the much-needed infrastructure upgrade.[245] The scale of the infrastructure upgrade was massive; its size was one of the reasons the project had never got off the ground. With federal dollars involved, it gained new life. The planning involved creating a 4,400-foot bridge across a large span of open water. A 45-foot drawbridge was added to the design to accommodate boat traffic, and the structure would rest about 12 feet above the water, be 18 feet wide and accommodate both foot passengers and automobiles. The bridge foundation was a particular engineering and logistical challenge and involved hundreds of thousands of square footage of stone, gravel and fill.[246] It was an opportunity to employ a lot of people. Part of the vision also involved building an adequate modern road connecting the bridge to Route 7 in Swanton.

Construction of the original Missisquoi Bay Bridge between Swanton and Alburgh. *Image courtesy of the Swanton Historical Society.*

Everything fell into line, and a public works grant was awarded. Government officials immediately used the Works Progress Administration unemployment rolls to hire workers from Franklin County. The first stage involved about seventy-five workers; later stages required over two hundred.[247] Another infrastructure project at this time was the construction of the sewage disposal plant in St. Albans.[248]

Planners originally hoped the construction might be complete by the end of 1936, but there were inevitable delays. Bad weather also postponed work, causing engineering difficulties. The effort stretched out into 1937 with its completion in sight. As it came together, the drawbridge was installed.[249] Unfortunately, accidents occurred. With so much going on, accidents were bound to happen. In November 1937, Roland Rochon was killed while working on the East Alburgh section, where heavy equipment and trucks constantly ran. While standing next to one of the dump trucks, the fill beneath his feet gave way. The truck was dragged into the hole on top of him.[250] In early 1938, cost overruns hit. With almost everything nearly complete, the state needed a little more money to get it finished.[251] Another death occurred when Henry Jones, a supervising engineer, contracted pneumonia. He died in the middle of February in the St. Albans hospital.[252]

The bridge temporally opened in early 1938. When the source of the final funding was in doubt, the bridge was closed, to the frustration of many. Finally, on Sunday, April 10, all was completed. The funding and payment plan were in order. The Missisquoi Bay Bridge was up and running.

The federal effort to get people back to work was more expansive than is commonly known today. Due to agricultural and economic interests, much of Vermont had been deforested. One of the first work initiatives came in March 1932 with a massive tree-planting program. The entire state took part. Locally, businesses in Highgate participated and ordered over ten thousand white and red pine trees. St. Albans planted close to one thousand trees of different types.[253] Other area municipalities got involved, and by September, Franklin County had planted nearly twenty-six thousand trees.[254] The following year, hundreds of men were hired to do forestry work, primarily in other regions of the state.

Employment opportunities were consistent, the work was reasonable and the public seemed satisfied with the results. Perry H. Merrill, the state forester, planned to expand these early efforts. He wanted to promote Vermont's scenic beauty and provide public access to isolated mountains, lakes and streams.[255] Soon, his department had organized nineteen Vermont Forest Conservation Camps with three thousand workers. As dollars flowed in, Franklin County was advised to develop more projects or it would miss out. In short order, the development of Bellevue Hill and the beach in St. Albans Bay Park were planned. Additional ideas were quickly under consideration, including support for the Chester A. Arthur birthplace in Fairfield and mountain parks in Montgomery and Bakersfield.[256] Work on Hazen's Notch was also a possibility, seen as a strong benefit to the county's eastern towns. Agencies used the winter as planning time, and by the late spring of 1934, Vermont governor Stanely Wilson toured St. Albans Bay, giving area projects an immediate stamp of approval. Soon, forty men worked on clearing a recreational road on the 1,400-foot-high Bellevue Hill, and the final plans were in place for the St. Albans Bay Park.[257] The Bellevue Hill project expanded, needing a team of forty-three men. They constructed a road for automobiles that was about one mile long and created a parking area and an overlook. When done, the men were moved to assist those working at the bay. Also in 1934, the West Berkshire border crossing station on Route 108 was constructed.[258]

All did not go as planned. St. Albans officials were a little slow in accepting some federal aid. They were urged by Merrill to apply for aid with some undeveloped initiatives, and as late as July 1935, sixty-four WPA projects had been approved in Vermont. None were in St. Albans. Two smaller endeavors in Richford and Enosburg had already received the go-ahead.[259] As of September 1935, state and local officials considered transferring the St. Albans workmen elsewhere. City officials worked to play catch-up. Soon, four or five work sites had been approved for the city.

Meanwhile, other initiatives were pitched and approved. Crews had already worked on upgrades to the county courthouse, Coote Field and Bellows Free Academy in St. Albans. The same crews were slated to upgrade the water lines in the area of Lake, Federal and Kingman Streets. They were also to clean, drain and flush the existing sewer system in the city and complete street improvements in other locations.[260]

By August, most of the organizational kinks had been ironed out, and four local governments were able to take advantage of Roosevelt's newest WPA funding measure. Work included a playground for the Enosburg school, gravel and culverts for two miles of road in Highgate, roof repairs for two Montgomery schools and maintenance on a school in St. Albans.[261] The money was not done coming in. A separate program brought more employment. Sheldon received funds for four miles of road construction. Swanton got approval for more trees. Georgia completed five miles of roadwork. Montgomery received funding for road reconstruction and two small bridges.[262] Bakersfield formalized a request for new fire hydrants. And the Morses Line border crossing in Franklin was built.[263]

And WPA money continued to pour in. More local projects got the go-ahead from President Roosevelt. There had been numerous automobile accidents on the town line between Georgia and St. Albans, where the Central Vermont line intersected with the main road. The railroad company, the state and local officials all agreed that there was a problem but disagreed about which entity should pay for the improvements. With the arrival of federal dollars, an overpass above the tracks was constructed. Other allotments funded road improvements at Sheldon Junction and two small projects in Swanton and St. Albans.[264]

The support for local projects continued. The town of Fairfield was given approval to work on its school buildings. Federal monies helped repaint classrooms during vacations. New windows were installed.[265]

The federal government initiated a cost-of-living survey in June 1936. It was similar to the Census Bureau's efforts. The Agricultural Experimentation Station at UVM and the WPA administered the program. Ninety-two personnel went door-to-door in communities throughout the Green Mountains. Special emphasis was placed on collecting data from farms. Swanton and Richford were two of the communities surveyed.[266] Swanton was awarded more WPA funds for expanding waterlines and creating sidewalks. Improvements were made to Alumni Field in the village.

In 1937, the Works Progress Administration built the St. Albans grade school and finished improvements to the athletic field at the high school.

The old brick border station at Morses Line in Franklin. *Photo by Armand Messier and Northern Vermont Aerial Photography.*

In 1938, the old Georgia Town Hall was restored to its original 1800 appearance. A large dedication ceremony was held, with the governor and many other public officials attending.[267]

In 1939, the county received more economic benefits from the New Deal. Originally part of an older building, the sugaring murals in the current St. Albans Post Office were completed. The National Treasury Section of Fine Arts funded the culturally significant art display.[268]

Other initiatives involved facilities at the Canadian border and continued into the 1940s. In Highgate, near the eastern shores of Missisquoi Bay, an international border crossing station was completed.[269] In Richford, upgrades were made to the border station operating in the north section of town, and the Public Works Administration completed a small dam.[270]

The projects were designed to get Americans back to work, to put paychecks in people's wallets and to provide critical infrastructure that improved the lives of all in the community. The New Deal defined and demonstrated the federal government's commitment to saving the economy by ensuring work opportunities for citizens. People needed to have jobs for the economy to get going again.

Much of this history is still used and enjoyed today, but its origins in Roosevelt's New Deal are often not recognized. Many of these structures, locations and sites are still around.

They tell the story of how the federal government helped Franklin County get through the Great Depression.

Chapter Seventeen

The Cold War
in Franklin County

I t is difficult for people who never lived through certain eras to understand how times have changed. When one has not directly witnessed or wrestled with the past, it is impossible to replicate the feelings and tensions associated with certain events. One such situation was the threat of nuclear war.

Documentaries, books and lesson plans cover grand events, but new generations might not realize that local spots are woven into the national narrative. People see the "Big Golf Ball" just east of St. Albans. Younger folks, not understanding the importance of that structure, gave it that name. Older generations knew all about that radar tower. The other major Cold War site is the former nuclear missile silo in Swanton. Many have heard about it, but fifty years later, few citizens know much about it. These two sites were part of the military machine that would have been called on had the Cold War boiled into a hot war. The unthinkable is that those locations are linked to events that literally threatened the existence of the human race.

First, a little perspective.

Vermonters think of themselves as far from the center of the universe. Despite Montreal, Boston and New York being just a few hours away, the Green Mountains have maintained a vista of forestland, farm fields and small towns. How the area became intricately linked to the Cold War is an interesting story.

The Soviet Union and the United States were not on the best of terms after World War II. The relationship between the former allies soured because of stark differences between democratic capitalism and totalitarian communism. Both sides deployed nuclear weapons and other new military technologies at an alarming pace.

Franklin County had a small part to play in events unfolding on the world stage.

One location to receive attention was the National Guard Motor Vehicle Storage Building on Lower Newton Road in St. Albans. It was constructed in 1949, just four years after the end of World War II, when tensions between East and West began to boil over. The U.S. Army Corps of Engineers designed the building.[271]

As problems with the Soviet Union increased and aircraft and missile technology improved, the United States developed systems to protect assets at home. The biggest military base in the region was the U.S. Air Force base in Plattsburgh, New York. It was huge, and in the 1950s, it needed an advanced radar network of scanning equipment. Part of the network was built in St. Albans on one of the highest points in Franklin County and became what some locals refer to as the "Golf ball."

It was a major investment to keep the country safe. In 1951, the military selected a location near Plattsburgh that would most benefit the newest radar systems. Elevation was a key factor, so Bellevue Hill was selected.[272] Its purpose was to monitor unidentified aircraft nearing American and allied airspace. A secondary part of the base's mission was to guide American aircraft to any approaching targets. As with all technology, advancements happened fast and furiously. By 1958, some of the first upgrades had been made to the sensing equipment. The next year, another round of improvements was made, with more in 1960. Further upgrades were made in 1962 and 1963.

The other significant Cold War–era addition to Franklin County was the Atlas Missile Base in Swanton. It wasn't unique. It was part of the defense system for the Plattsburgh Airforce Base, one of several to be built around the military airport. Often, when something is produced, other, better technologies are waiting in the wings. Advancements can become obscure pretty quickly. This was the case with the missiles constructed as part of the "Ring of Fire" around Plattsburgh. By the time the silos were in the ground and the missiles were in place, the U.S. military had moved on. Better tech called for moving U.S. missiles to mobile units and submarines.

But none of that diminishes Swanton's unique Cold War–era history.

Construction on the site began in June 1960. Many of the workers were local men who had served in the military. One was Armand Messier, who

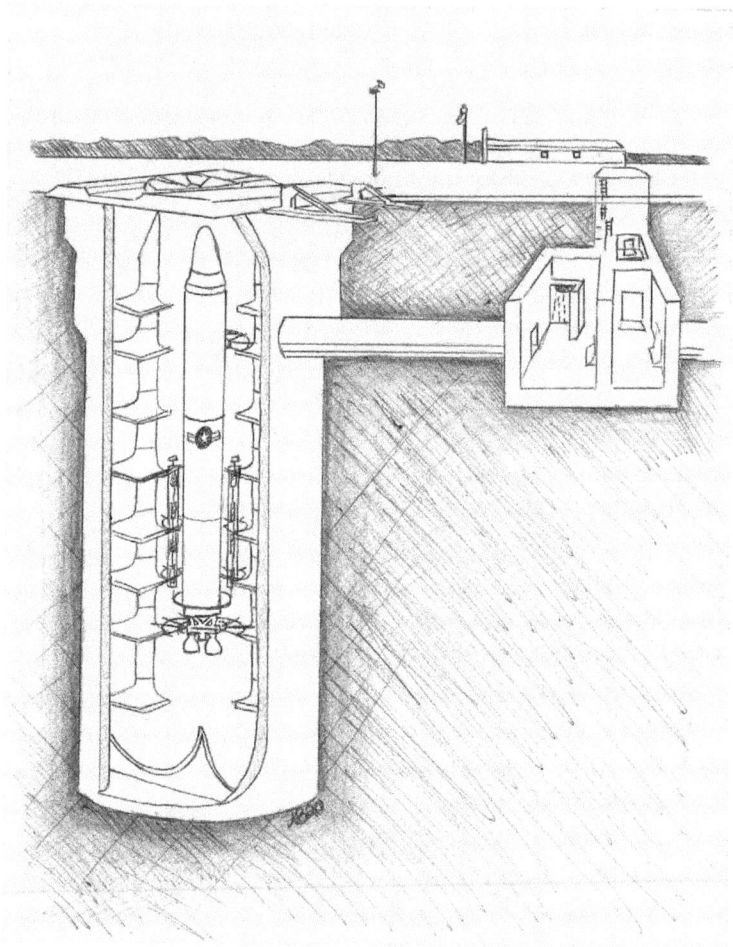

Diagram of the Atlas missile silos constructed in Swanton and Alburgh. *Artwork by Ashley Bowen.*

served as a missile field mechanic. Crews dug down 180 feet and erected a ground silo hole 55 feet in diameter. Messier recalled that the first few feet at the construction site were dirt but that the rest of the effort involved blasting shale and removing it. Completing the silo involved severe accidents. Sadly, there were two fatal mishaps.[273]

The missile was known as an Atlas ICBM (intercontinental ballistic missile) and was different than anything Franklin County had ever seen. Just getting it into small-town Vermont was an engineering accomplishment. It was flown into Plattsburgh Airforce Base on July 26, 1962. It weighed eight tons and was placed on a specially built tractor-trailer bed. The New York State Police, the Vermont State Police and U.S. Air Force personnel were involved in escorting it to its destination. It entered Vermont from the Rouses Point bridge, traveling at a cautious ten to thirty miles per hour. The load was so large that on Route 78 through Alburgh, the telephone wires needed to be pushed up with extension poles. Another Atlas missile went up in Alburgh.

The missile sites were in operation for only three years. The silos were operated at a critical point in human history. As they came online, they quickly went to the highest possible alert status, as America was plunged into the Cuban Missile Crisis. Throughout 1962, the Soviet Union had tried to get its own missiles deployed in Cuba to counter any aggression by the United States. America's hands were not clean when it came to Cuba, with the failed Bay of Pigs invasion only months before. Weeks passed, and more Soviet ships approached the Caribbean Sea. The Soviet government claimed that it was providing the Cuban people with defensive weapons. The American government monitored the buildup and became concerned. On October 22, President John F. Kennedy addressed the American people. He told the country about the Russian nuclear missiles and then established a blockade of the tiny island nation.

The world had never been so close to nuclear war.

In the backwoods of Swanton, crews manned the Atlas missile. These men were a small part of the chain of command that held the fate of the world in their hands. Armand Messier recalled reporting for duty during third shift during the October crisis. As a field mechanic, he spent most of his time in one of the base's Quonset huts. Those buildings had been used as storage and maintenance during construction. He recalled that the missile crews actually lived underground in the silo, in the crew quarters, which were just above the control center of the base.[274] During the crisis, extra security guards and guard dogs were stationed around the perimeter.

The crisis waned. Locals went on with their lives.

The old radar tower in St. Albans. *Photo by Armand Messier and Northern Vermont Aerial Photography.*

And the Cold War continued.

The Swanton base experienced a bit of international espionage as well. In April 1963, just six months after the Cuban Missile Crisis, a Soviet agent passed through the area, attempting to gather information about the complex. His name was Kaarlo Rudoph Tuomi, and he had been forwarding American military secrets to Soviet intelligence. His work involved traveling to the area and collecting information disguised as a fisherman.[275]

By January 20, 1965, the decision had been made to dismantle the sites. New technology had developed that fast. The United States embraced a more mobile nuclear capability, and having stationary missile silos was no longer a good investment. Things moved so quickly that, by August 1966, the land where the silo was located, on Middle Road not far from the Missisquoi River, had gone up for sale. Less than a decade after the silo's construction, the federal government completely washed its hands of the endeavor.

Chapter Eighteen

The Franklin Commune and Other Hippie Colonies

I t may be a bit awkward for some to acknowledge, but Vermont was a utopia for the counterculture movement fifty years ago. Even more interesting is the fact that quiet, isolated and traditional Franklin County was a dream destination for countless hippies.

The Vietnam War raged. Men who didn't want to go to war were being drafted. The civil rights movement inspired millions. John F. Kennedy, Martin Luther King and Robert Kennedy had been assassinated. Man walked on the moon. The Beatles, the Doors, Pink Floyd and the Rolling Stones produced memorable music. The generation that came of age during these events saw Vermont as the place to be.

It was a different time.

And the memories of that period are being lost. Participants who are still around are entering their eighth decade. Some have passed on.

In 2016, the Vermont Historical Society captured elements of the era with its exhibit "Hippies, Freaks, and Radicals." Oral histories were conducted. Pictures were shared. Forums were held.

Those efforts, while appropriate, only scratched the surface of the counterculture presence in Vermont. Franklin County, with its conservative small-town nature, got some appropriate exposure. However, the history here was overshadowed by activity in other regions. Some who lived on communes in Windham County wrote books about their experiences. Other communes got statewide exposure based on events of the day.

The property in Franklin that was home to the "Earthworks" Commune. *Courtesy of Larry Mead.*

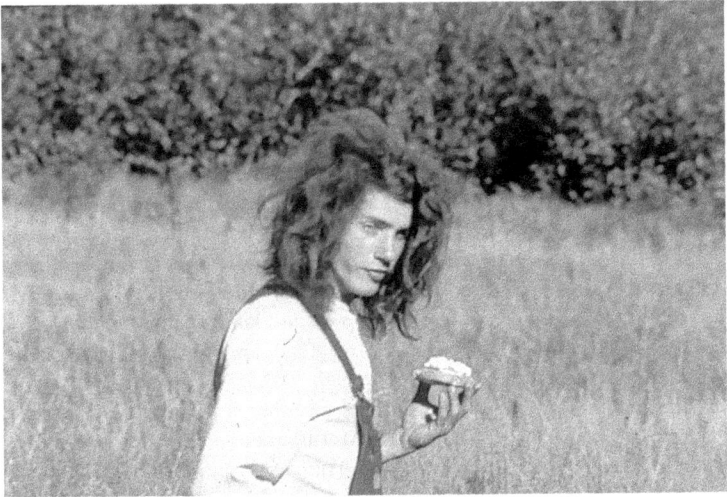

Charlie Pratt taught at UVM and was one of the original Franklin Commune members. *Courtesy of Larry Mead.*

And some people in quiet little Franklin County want to forget that the hippies were ever here.

The story of the counterculture in northwestern Vermont should not remain hidden.

The kids of the sixties, despite some radical political beliefs, came to Franklin County and bravely embraced ideals most local people claim to live by. Despite their knowledge of Chairman Mao, Karl Marx and Vladimir Lenin, the "back to the landers" cared for one another, helped their neighbors and attended town meetings. They shunned American capitalism and pushed back against racism, the Vietnam War and other ills of society. But they ended up here, in our little corner of Vermont.

Nearly every Franklin County town had a bit of a hippie presence. Against this backdrop were local families that had paid the ultimate sacrifice. Vermont boys, barely out of high school, served in Vietnam. Several died there. While locals watched antiwar protests spread across the country on the evening news, the newcomers worked farm fields once owned by area families. The situation was offensive to some.

Their presence is best defined by the number of locations they settled. So many places were occupied by the hippies that the content and stories would take up an encyclopedia volume. The idealistic young people began to pop up in the Green Mountains in the late 1960s. Just a few years later, the counterculture was in full bloom. By early 1970, one estimate revealed that as many as 35,800 had arrived.[276] On the low end, one estimate had just over fifty communes in Vermont.[277] Some college professors speculated that the number was much higher, closer to two hundred.

The most significant local presence was the Franklin Commune. It was a radical group even compared to all of the others settling in Vermont. Jim and Barbara Nolfi and Bruce Taub and Mary Pat Palmer moved from California in the summer of 1969. Jim Nolfi had a teaching job at UVM. A wealthy Californian had agreed to purchase land for the creation of a commune and wanted to support new revolutionary lifestyles.[278] After some consideration, they agreed on a 350-acre farm that was for sale in Franklin. In Burlington, the group encountered Charlie Pratt and Mary Louise Andrews. Friends Peter and Shannon McFarland also agreed to participate in the venture. A newcomer was Peter Hutcher. A number of the couples brought their children. A highly educated group, many of the members had advanced college degrees. Their reading interests included such material as Henry David Thoreau's *Walden*, B.F. Skinner's *Walden Two*, Helen and Scott Nearing's *The Good Life* and Chairman Mao's "Little Red Book."[279]

At the start of 1970, the group published a radical newspaper, the *Vermont Railroad*, and disseminated it to area colleges and schools. The paper was so inflammatory to some traditionalists that an investigation was demanded on the floor of the Vermont Senate. Since Nolfi and Pratt worked at UVM, some members of the Vermont House wanted to cut funding to the college.[280]

The new arrivals could not have cared less about the stir they caused. They moved onto the property in late winter and quickly immersed themselves in "back to the land" projects. In February, March and April, they sugared for the first time. The commune effort received the nickname "Earthworks," as the members purchased a cow for milking and a team of horses.[281] Franklin resident George Truax helped them become comfortable handling the horses and using the sugaring equipment. It was a big learning experience. They found nearly three thousand sap buckets in the barn and were willing to learn. Some friendly locals did help them out. They taught them how to put taps in the trees, how to hang buckets and how to get enough wood for the season. Locals were not above playing the occasional prank on the somewhat naive but very eager new arrivals. In one instance, they walked with the communards through a thick area of maples. Every tree was tapped, and they got to the road. Like any parent addressing a

The Franklin Commune embraced a "back to the land" mentality. That effort involved working with many different farm animals. *Courtesy of Larry Mead.*

youngster, the hippies were told to follow directions and just get the job done. In so doing, the longtime residents had the hippies tap everything, including a telephone pole.

In April and May, the commune's residents prepared a two-acre garden plot designed to grow enough food for all of the families to subsist on for most of the winter. By June, they were engaged in radical political activity again, entering an antiwar float in the Enosburg Dairy Day Parade. Members brought guns with them but decorated the firearms with blooming wildflowers.[282]

In the late spring, the constant news of American deaths in Vietnam hit home for the people of Franklin County. George Edward Walker Jr. of Swanton was killed on May 26 by an explosive device. He was a medical specialist for the U.S. Army. He perished in the Chuong Thien Province.[283]

Many who lived on the Franklin Commune came with their families. Their children were raised on the property. *Courtesy of Larry Mead.*

This sort of devastating news for locals explains why some might have harbored ill feelings toward the hippies living in the woods.

On the farm, though, they worked just as hard as old-time Vermonters. They spent their peak summer days working outside, just like Franklin County farmers. They planted, weeded, hoed and mulched. During the dry weather of June and July, they feared that a lack of rain would kill their crops. They gardened, sometimes naked, and grew cabbages, corn, potatoes, tomatoes and the other staple crops that Vermonters cultivate.

In response to the youth movement that had spread across the country, on July 1, the Twenty-Sixth Amendment to the U.S. Constitution was adopted. The voting age was lowered from twenty-one to eighteen.

Some positive relationships grew between locals and the commune. At some point, Grace and Kenneth Spooner, who owned a farm to the southwest of the Franklin Commune, asked for help. The couple was elderly and needed assistance getting all of their hay in. They feared summer thunderstorms and knew there were able-bodied youngsters capable of getting the job done. About an hour later, in the blazing afternoon heat, Charlie Pratt, Bruce Taub and many others were doing the neighborly Vermont thing, providing a helping hand. For a job well done, the Spooners offered thirst-quenching lemonade.

Among the experiments in true alternative living, old school buses were used as housing. And in true hippie fashion, multiple people often crashed in those buses. Peter McFarland, one of the originals who had a good amount of skill with his hands, constructed living quarters for he and his wife. It was a small, mobile, enclosed wagon that others soon dubbed the "Gypsy Cart."

The true measure of a successful growing season is the quantity and quality of the produce. In this regard, the output of the communards may have equaled the most seasoned, successful old-timer. They had planted so many tomato plants that the garden was full of the big, juicy fruit. There was so much produce that they had to contact other communes in the area to see if people were willing to come up and lend a hand. From late July through August and September, the group proudly hosted visitors who already embraced the giving and sharing lifestyle of the 1960s. Squads of hippies descended into the rows of tomatoes for weeks. Bushels were collected. As the produce was brought in, the canning began. They learned how to sanitize jars in boiling water. Next, the tomatoes were heated to peel off the skins. Jars were tightly packed, and air bubbles were poked out. Youngsters then waited for the rewarding sucking pop, confirming that the old tradition had been done right. With the task completed, the jars were stored in the basement for the approaching winter.

The Franklin Commune's leadership relevance played out in September 1970, when it hosted the "Gathering of the Tribes" on the weekend of the fall equinox. Many hippies and longhairs from around Vermont visited for a working couple of days. They helped at various farm-related tasks but also engaged in organization meetings. The entire event was arranged to bring the plethora of hippie colonies, collectives and communes together. It wasn't just a big party. The discussions held on the Franklin property lead to local food co-ops and the health clinic in Burlington. Estimates vary from at least several dozen to well over one hundred participants. The larger number is probably more accurate. The amount of work that went into the event was considerable. Members traveled to other communes to promote the event.

Work responsibilities on the Franklin Commune were often planned and organized in advance. On this day, the men entertained the kids. *Courtesy of Larry Mead.*

On the final nights of the "Gathering," there was a fall chill to the air. The meeting was like no other seen in northern Vermont. The attendees needed food and meals, so members of a commune called Myrtle Hill helped the Franklinites prepare enough food. They chopped onions and potatoes and prepared stews of rice and veggies, cooked over an open fire pit and was deliciously warm against the coming cold.[284] On the last night, many of the attendees gathered around a bonfire, linked arms and sang the words, "Wearing my long wing feathers I fly, I circle around, the boundaries of the Earth."[285] Counterculture icon Ravi Shankar sat on the front porch of the farmhouse. The performer graced the rolling hills of northwest Vermont with the inviting sounds of quiet revolution and social change.[286]

The war in Vietnam went on, and another local young man lost his life. Chief Petty Officer Carroll Joseph Deuso was killed in a non-combat-related air crash off the coast of North Vietnam's Kien Haa Province.[287]

The story of the Franklin Commune continued through 1971, '72 and '73. During the winters, typically only some of the core members remained. They tended to the animals, maintained the property and prepared for the next sugaring season. The snows came and went. The cold temperatures let go, and the ground thawed. The spring of 1971 proved another successful sugaring season. Mud season came and went. Summer was right around the corner, and once again, the back-to-the-land atmosphere dominated the property. At times, there was so much work that the commune hosted dozens of visitors. Some were committed to helping out with the project, others passed the time with drugs. Summer warmth blessed the participants, and there was more naked gardening. Fall arrived, and there was more canning and food preservation.

The utopian endeavor took a hit on November 23, 1971.

A fire destroyed the main house. The fire was a significant local event and was covered in both of the Franklin County newspapers. They reported that the Franklin Fire Department had responded to the call and that only four adults were present at the time.[288] The children were safe, and no one was hurt, but a lot of human labor and effort went up in flames with the building.

A few months passed, and many of the original communards considered departing. During the winter and early spring, many of them had stuck it out, working on the construction of a new building. The building, however, was unfinished, and constructing it in the cold proved to be a physically and mentally exhausting task. Over the spring and summer of 1972, most of the original communards decided to depart. Newer members looked to carry on the effort. People still worked on and visited the commune through the late fall of 1973.

While the story of the Franklin effort is the most prominent, it was far from the only home to hippies. The term *commune* is relative. One resident may have thought they were investing in a communal effort, another may have identified as participating in something totally different. There were also squatters and drifters. The hippie presence was prevalent enough that on December 7, 1970, the *Saint Albans Messenger* ran a front-page story noting the existence of at least six communes in area towns. Franklin had been up and running, but others were in Montgomery, Bakersfield, Enosburg Falls, Fairfield and Fairfax. Another source identified one in Fletcher. Most of these remain mysterious, lost to the passage of time.

The Montgomery effort was notable. The commune was located fairly close to the village. The road on which it was founded is now named Dreamer Lane. The group didn't try to attract attention, but many people visited.

People from other communes came to help the Franklin Commune rebuild. A fire destroyed its farmhouse in the winter of 1971. *Courtesy of Larry Mead.*

The Montgomery folks were seen as having very high aspirations. However, many of those lofty goals tended to be gone as quickly as a dream, hence the name the "Dreamers." They gardened enough food to put some away in the winter and built a cabin in the woods. By the middle of the 1970s, most of the commune members had departed. Montgomery attracted different groups on various properties. A few were random squatters in the woods. Others lived in abandoned farmhouses for short periods of time.

Then there is the story of woodland property in Fairfield. Other people were involved, but Meta Strick has been living on the same property for fifty years now. Earlier in life, she worked in human services in Buffalo, New York. She and her first husband, considering all of the cracks forming in society, decided to move to Vermont in 1968. Eventually, she settled down in her new home, but like so many of America's young citizens, her personal views of what the United States was going through greatly impacted her own choices.[289] During the same months in 1971 that Meta Strick started living in the woods on her new property, the state of Vermont was concerned about thousands of college kids, dropouts and transients joining Vermont's commune movement. She moved onto the ninety-acre plot of land with a small group. With her husband and small child, they lived out of her car and a tent during the first summer in the woods. During the first winter, they moved into the basement of the unfinished log cabin they were building. When spring and summer arrived again, further improvements were made to the land. However, every time she took the family for a natural bath down at Fairfield Pond, she ended up being scorned by locals.

The state of Vermont was well aware of the societal ripples created by so many wandering youth and began to publicly debate ways to make the Green Mountains less appealing to outsiders. On April 14, 1971, the *Messenger* reported that two Vermont state senators were concerned about another hippie influx. They were exploring ways of making residency a requirement for someone receiving state benefits.[290] In other words, if you were part of the counterculture and drifting through the area just to see what all of the commotion was about and expected a free lunch, you had to move on.

Meta didn't. She worked as a social worker in the community and raised her children here.

Fifty years on, Meta's property easily measures against the longevity of some locals.

Another group was in East Fairfield, and it was effectively a musicians' colony. The appearance of several musicians, unplanned, in the backwoods of the county may appear random. But artistic types always have a way of finding one another. These unique individuals practiced their craft, formed bands and played at venues across the state.

One of the more interesting incidents of the era happened on Saturday night, April 29, 1971. The *Messenger* picked up on the news and couldn't resist reporting it. With temperatures not quite warm enough to forget winter, a group of hippies from an area commune rushed to the St. Albans hospital with a very pregnant young woman. Despite having embraced nature in uncommon ways, she wanted a healthcare professional to assist with the birth. However, after arriving in the parking lot in the dark of night, the moment of truth approached. The attending doctor insisted that the birth happen inside, where sanitation was not a problem and medications were readily available. At first, the hippies refused, wanting their friend to deliver in the great outdoors. When the labor pains increased and the mother needed to be moved to a hospital bed, the hippies asked if the child could be named "Swamp Grass."[291]

On May 6, 1971, the *Saint Albans Messenger* again misconstrued and overreported the "threat" that the youth represented. National political events were running hot because of the Vietnam War, and local authorities were

HIDDEN HISTORY OF FRANKLIN COUNTY, VERMONT

nervous about radicals. The Vermont Electric Company, which had been contacted by authorities because of an unspecific threat to the substation in Highgate, decided to employee private security. As in the summer of 1970, the state was bracing for another hippie epidemic and still trying to figure out how to deal with the ones who had already settled in. The paper went out of its way to point out that "dangerous radicals" could be in the area and posed a direct threat to the power station.[292] To the best of anyone's recollection, no threats emerged.

All of this doesn't include the French Hill Commune, which may have been the county's most visible, as it was located just east of St. Albans City. It had pigs and maple sugaring, and its residents enjoyed life to the fullest. The effort started in 1971, when Jim Collins, his wife, Susannah, and several others purchased land near where the Town Forest is today. Others joined, like Mike Palmer, who at one point had been living in a tent in Enosburg. When he settled in the commune he was already living in a cabin at the top of French Hill. Mike took up beekeeping and today is a well-known commercial honey producer.

A summation of what happened in the county cannot be complete without discussing the most public—and most shameful—episode involving law enforcement, locals and hippies. A fellow by the name of Otto Kremer, who had moved to the county and like so many others and became involved in social justice causes, opened a hippie hangout in St. Albans in 1973. Kremer was involved with a survey at BFA (Bellows Free Academy), where youth were asked questions about sexuality and their views on communal living. Many locals didn't appreciate the information-gathering effort. The establishment he started on Main Street in St. Albans was Tuner's. It was designed to appeal to those who had moved into the area and the local youth who were emulating them. Locals were not impressed, especially a local businessman, Keith Campbell, whose office was located between Tuner's and another hippie establishment just down the street. To some, there were legitimate concerns about the type, quality and look of the people hanging out in Taylor Park. Locals associated the long hair and the dirty clothing with drugs and the worst of society. For the most part, that perception was a gross mischaracterization of the counterculture. Kramer's establishment was meant to welcome those who were loitering, and he even organized cleanup patrols in the park.

Perhaps affected by years of anti-Vietnam protests on television, maybe calloused by the deaths of Franklin County boys in Vietnam, locals were all too quick to try to squash the presence of the counterculture. There was a perception at the time, at least among law enforcement, elected officials and many families, that marijuana was a very bad drug. They believed it was part of a group of addictive substances that led to hard drug use and ruined lives. In response, the St. Albans City Council voted to bring in an undercover police officer to deal with the hippie kids and the drugs in the area.

The officer was Paul Lawrence, and his legacy puts a dark exclamation point on how some locals felt about the hippie colonies and the communes in the backwoods.

Lawrence started working in St. Albans during the late summer of 1973 and, while undercover, identified members of the counterculture who were part of the drug trade. Lawrence had been a state trooper and worked in several other jurisdictions.

Starting with something called "The 2nd St. Albans Raid," he fed information to the state police, the county sheriff and the St. Albans Police Department about an out-of-control heroin and cocaine problem. On October 24, thirty police officers were involved in drug raids across the county. More than two dozen people were arrested, and warrants were issued for the arrest of several others. Most were brought up on heroin and cocaine charges.[293] Most of these charges were later dismissed, and Paul Lawrence was later convicted of perjury.

The damage had been done. And the small-town bias against the hippies had been embarrassingly exposed.

This fascinating history is hidden by half a century of elapsed time. The tensions and growing pains that America went through in the 1960s and '70s happened all over the place. For the residents of Franklin County, most of it was viewed from comfortable living rooms while watching the evening news. Local men and women answered the call and served in a war that not everyone back home believed in. The resistance to that war became so vast that America's youth sought out isolated places like Vermont.

In general, the nation has come a long way in appropriately collecting the stories of Vietnam veterans. They sacrificed more than most will ever know. Rightly or wrongly, their nation called, and they did their jobs. Many of these veterans lost friends in the jungles of Vietnam and still bear the scars.

A completely honest analysis of history also examines those youth who rebelled against the draft, the war and the actions of their government. Many of them came to our little corner of Vermont.

Their stories are unique, powerful and, unfortunately, still mostly hidden.

Chapter Nineteen

"We Could Lose the Whole Town"

The Swanton Fire of 1970

B ig events that affect an entire region are not supposed to happen. Small-town America gets up every morning and goes to work. The pages on the calendar turn. The years pass.

So, when an event happens that remains in the community's collective consciousness, it is big. Such is the case with the Swanton Fire of 1970. For those alive at the time, it was a watershed community moment. It is rare, when considering local events, for so many residents to vividly recall a single date.

Merchants Row in Swanton is the long commercial block just east of the bridge over the Missisquoi River. In today's America of big-box stores, this block feels like it belongs to a different era. The buildings are too long and impressive to be related to the strip malls of the 1980s. Over the decades, different businesses have occupied the spaces. Different generations can recall shopping at the small independent shops. Visitors mark the spot's scenic beauty, with the falls of the Missisquoi River nearby. A historic village green features a gazebo, monuments, plenty of summer shade and a chance for a quick walk. Elders have names for close landmarks nearby: Gristmill Hill and Marble Mill.

The location is not without problems. The truck traffic in that stretch is among the heaviest in the state. Parking is a major issue, with shoppers's cars tightly sharing spots. Uncounted vehicles navigate the snakelike turns in Route 78. It is a location that nearly every local has visited.

And if they are old enough, they can recall the cold January evening that destroyed Merchants Row.

At the time, the businesses were the economic anchors any community would want: Pearl's Department Store, Robert Horton's Insurance Agency, Swanton Rexall Drugs, Parah's Antique and Furniture Store, Ben Franklin, Taylor Marine, the B&L Gift Shop. Across the river was Swanton Lumber.

On January 28, 1970, a massive fire altered the landscape of Swanton and gutted Merchants Row, the heart of the village's downtown.

Snow covered the ground. The wind was strong, with gusts of over forty miles per hour. No one really knows how the fire started. Shortly before 11:00 p.m., Eugene Gokey came home from work. His apartment was on the second floor of the southernmost portion of Merchants Row. His neighbor was Roy Hemingway. They both smelled smoke. It wasn't like the whiff from a campfire or the smell of burning brush. This was thick, as though a lot of different things were on fire. Peeking through the windows of Parah's, they saw flames. The powerful winds were already wreaking havoc, fanning the fire inside. The two men rushed back to the apartments, set off the fire alarm and got other folks in the apartments to safety. Seeds of panic set in. What was happening was well out of the ordinary.

Any chance to prevent disaster passed in those first few moments. Less than fifteen minutes later, the Swanton Volunteer Fire Department was on the scene. What the first responders immediately saw spread doubts as to what could be saved. Fire Chief Donald Bell and his men noted that the fire had already burned most of Parah's and that flames were roaring through the front window.

If it had been a normal night, maybe the firemen could have beat the fire, saving Merchants Row. But the wind….

The gusts took hold of the blaze in the first store, and it was like a spark in a dry forest. Embers were everywhere, flames racing like a thousand angry hornets. Nine hoses were set on the inferno, but the weather was so bad that the water had little effect. The pressure was fine, but, because of the wind, the water was sprayed and thrown everywhere, including back at the firemen. The blaze was spreading. The enormity of the situation dawned on everyone. The entire Merchants Row block was in serious danger. There was even a risk to other parts of the village.

Back in the village offices, a plea for help went out. Village clerk David Blondo and others were on the radio and phones with other towns, pleading for assistance. As other town fire departments got the emergency call and responded, the Swanton Fire Department was helpless against the sheer size of what it faced.

Parah's store was fully engulfed. The windows had blown out. Flames reached into the sky and were tossed about in the wind. The water hoses pounded the block, but the Ben Franklin store was burning and Robert Horton's Insurance was being destroyed. The firemen tried, but it was David versus Goliath. In this case, the giant kept getting bigger.

Business owners rushed inside the untouched portions of their establishments, ahead of the flames, and tried to save anything. Spauldings, the owners of the drugstore, got most of their supply of medicines out of their pharmacy. Donald and Earl Taylor grabbed what they could from Taylor Marine. The owners of Pearl's Department Store rescued everything they could carry.

Other fire departments arrived: Highgate, Franklin and St. Albans.

The fire continued to spread. It was roaring so hard on Merchants Row that the first responders couldn't get within one hundred feet of the blaze. Hot embers had been blown clear across the river, where reports came in that Swanton Lumber was on fire. The entire village was at risk.

More departments arrived, but so many trucks and vehicles clogged the streets that not all of the equipment could be arranged to best fight the inferno. Since they were coming from the west, the crews from Isle la Motte,

Firemen struggle to contain the raging inferno. *Courtesy of the Swanton Historical Society.*

Crews battle the flames. *Courtesy of the Swanton Historical Society.*

Alburgh, North Hero and Grand Isle were called on to do battle on that side of the river. Reinforcements tried to save Swanton Lumber.

Further calls went out to towns in Upstate New York. Enosburg's fire department arrived. Canadian crews crossed the border to assist. The interstate was packed with trucks coming up from Winooski and Burlington.

At the peak of the effort to contain the blaze, more than twenty-one departments, three hundred firefighters and twenty-one pieces of equipment battled the inferno. The fear that it would spread down Canada Street or to one of the nearby residential blocks was a serious concern, and evacuations happened as a precaution. Ultimately, the fire jumped the street and burned Arthur Ledoux's apartment building.

County residents heard about their own departments answering the call and saw the glow of the blaze in Swanton illuminating the horizon. People who lived miles away looked west and saw a bright yellowish-orange haze against the night sky. Police set up traffic control at critical road junctions, moving bystanders away from the area. They helped the emergency crews navigate the clutter. The battle continued through the early-morning hours.

Finally, at about 4:00 a.m., the fire was under control. It wasn't out yet, but a sense of relief settled among the responders, knowing they had at least averted a worst-case scenario. Hours earlier, entire blocks of the village had been threatened. The loss of the business district was bad enough. Thankfully, people's homes were not destroyed.

Eight of Swanton's major buildings were scorched or destroyed. Eleven of the area's businesses claimed major losses. These included Hall's Hardware, Taylor Marine, Pearl's Department Store, Swanton Rexall, the Chittenden Trust Company, York Manufacturing in the old Taquahunga Club, Alfred Moreau's barbershop, Swanton Lumber, B&L Gift Shop, the Boucher Clothing Store and Ruby's Uniform Shop. Ten people had to find new places to live. Fifty had their places of work destroyed.

In the immediate aftermath, Swanton's downtown looked like a war zone. Smoldering boards belched wisps of smoke. Blackened piles of rubble were all that remained of prized buildings. A damp, smoky haze settled over the village green. The snow, now gray and black, looked like ashes from a campfire.

Over the course of the next several weeks, the community worked to recover. Governor Dean Davis toured the area. Repair crews spent time on damaged powerlines, making sure the rest of the village didn't suffer from the winter cold. Community members took in the displaced; neighboring towns sent clothing and supplies.

Repairs were made. Months passed. Eventually, Merchants Row was rebuilt and life moved on.

The event was so significant that in 2000, the Swanton Historical Society organized a thirty-year anniversary event. Local business owners were encouraged to tell their stories. Any of the brave firemen were asked to share their remembrances. It was well attended, and people's memories were crisp.

Other tributes followed. In 2010, a fortieth-anniversary event was held.

And on January 28, 2020, a fifty-year remembrance was organized. Townsfolk packed the village office. Firefighters—some in their seventies and a few in their eighties and nineties—were honored. Business owners retold their stories. Those who lived in Swanton Village and witnessed the fire offered their memories. The youth of the time, teenagers who looked out windows and witnessed the ominous orange glow in the village, shared their recollections.

CHAPTER TWENTY

"DOORS HONORING THE PAST"

The Historical Societies of Our Region

Some of our hidden history is out in the open for all to see. The historical societies of Franklin County are small, committed groups dedicated to capturing the history of the region. Each town has its own areas of interest, depending on the community's development. Mostly run by volunteers, these organizations are effectively community teachers and part-time museum curators. It is hard not to stop by one of these old buildings, receive a tour and feel as though you have just received "small town" hospitality. These people are proud of what they have collected. They are honored to share the identity of their Vermont towns.

BAKERSFIELD

Located near the center of the village, the organization uses the old Catholic church as its home. The building is eye-catching. Its three stories are impressive, the peaked stained-glass windows are striking and the pressed-tin white walls hint at historical religious purity. The members of the society have gone to great lengths to preserve different parts of the community's links to education, with very nice displays depicting Bakersfield Academy's history. Most of the interior is in amazing shape, with visitors wondering about the religious ceremonies of the past. A recent focus has been a fundraising drive to repair the area of the altar, which has not aged well.

BERKSHIRE

The Berkshire Historical Society is a real treat. It is an example of what a tiny town accomplishes when it preserves elements from its past. Its beautiful building is a little church not far from the Missisquoi River. That the society operates in one of the community's old sanctuaries is a great link to the past. Classic Vermont farm fields surround the site, and an old cemetery rests behind the building. Inside, a unique assortment of artifacts represents Berkshire's long history. From old musical instruments and nineteenth-century clothing, to photographs of important local residents, the society's efforts represent the best of historic preservation.

ENOSBURG

The Enosburg Historical Society is located in the center of the village. It has an emphasis on the region's train history, with a single section of rail and a striking orange caboose accessible to the public. This is a wonderful hook, as eager kids get the chance to explore how things used to be. The first room of the building features shelves full of reference books and old files. Those books are historical gold, and many of the folders hold the gems of Enosburg's story. Volunteers go the extra mile to make visitors feel at home and to create unique displays. A major feature is an exhibit focused on the town's medical history. Visitors get a vivid impression of the nineteenth century, when Enosburg boasted two patent-medicine companies. The fascinating array of tonic bottles that delivered "Missisquoi" products is hard to forget.

FAIRFIELD

Of all the societies in the county, Fairfield's is the most modern establishment. It is located in the town offices, in the center of the village. It maintains displays and collects artifacts in the "vault." The society has a significant collection of nineteenth-century tools that illustrate how much harder work was in the past. It is a unique piece of history, one that a very small number of towns across the nation can celebrate. The historical society also has the anchor of the President Chester Arthur Historic Site, birthplace of the twenty-first president of the United States.

FAIRFAX

As of the summer of 2020, substantial renovations were underway to repair and update the Fairfax Historical Society building. Its present home is prime property in the village and is a beautiful, historic structure. The society's collection is fun, accessible and charming. Tucked in between old tools, antique chairs and rare knickknacks is the town's original post office. It is quaint and inviting. Open antique mailboxes line the wall behind the desk. Other displays are just as much fun, including collections of old farm equipment. Early band uniforms show pride and honor locals who worked their way through the Fairfax school system.

FRANKLIN

One of the oldest historical societies in the county is in Franklin, and it has one of the most unique exhibits. Set in the middle of the village, the historic log cabin is what history is all about. Its worn wood exterior is unique among structures in the county and provides one of the best examples of what a local historical society can accomplish. Originally located in a different part of town, the building was acquired and then moved to its present location in 1992. Home to a few generations of Vermonters since it was built in

The Franklin Historical Society's old log cabin. *Photo by Armand Messier and Northern Vermont Aerial Photography.*

1877, it was purchased for preservation purposes in 1959. The cabin was repaired and restored. The interior provides a real picture of what life was like over one hundred years ago. How well would the walls have kept out the winter cold? How could an entire family live in such a small structure? The Franklin Historical Society allows you to imagine these things.

GEORGIA

The town's name originates from Vermont's long colonial history. When New Hampshire governor Benning Wentworth carved up plots of the Green Mountains, this land was named after the King of England. The Georgia Historical Society is in a great location on Route 7 and gets plenty of exposure. The town's historical society chapter started in 1975, when the old brick schoolhouse became available. Dating back to early in the twentieth century, it served as Georgia's one-room, multi-grade-level educational building for about sixty years. The society collection reflects the town's long history and the society's commitment to preserving the past.

HIGHGATE

The Highgate Historical Society is located in the center of town, on Route 78, near the old red-brick Methodist church. The facility features an extensive and well-maintained collection. On the first floor, visitors are greeted by old framed photographs and prominently featured farm and homestead equipment. Upstairs, the society has curated a wonderful amount of information that is easily accessible. More images line the walls, allowing visitors to investigate old businesses that operated in the town. The volunteers have captured how education once looked, as old photos depict former school buildings, sports teams and classrooms. The quality of artifacts is better than anything a teacher could access from a textbook. The members are eager to share their knowledge of the collection.

MONTGOMERY

The Montgomery Historical Society lies on Route 118 in St. Bartholomew's Church. It resides in a community that features several covered bridges and picturesque views of mountains. An unsolved mystery among the historical society members is the possibility that the current church was built over the old foundation of another, unknown building. The structure first received major renovations at some point after the Civil War, when the tower and Gothic features were added. The historical society was born in 1973, and its baptism involved efforts to buy and restore the abandoned building. It features large stained-glass windows, an impressive high front tower and original hand-hewn beams. The Montgomery Historical Society's building may be the most beautiful and memorable in the county.

RICHFORD

The Richford Historical Society was formed in 1978 and is housed in the 1908 fire station. It is located on Main Street, in the center of the village. The collection is kept on two floors of the old building. The ground floor contains a collection of historic photographs. There is an old horse-drawn wagon. Parts of the collection feature quaint advertising from old businesses. Visitors can glean how former products were marketed. Features of the original firehouse were kept intact. Upstairs, the preservation effort is a little more "homey," with a 1950s kitchen. The Richford Historical Society does a fine job at preserving its history.

SHELDON

The Sheldon Historical Society recently moved to a newly renovated historic building just east of the village. The structure was originally a store. It burned in a 1932 fire that also destroyed the Dead Creek covered bridge. The society's recent work has been impressive. One wall displays a museum timeline. Some photos show the original incarnations of the present building. Others proudly show the recent renovation work. All depict a committed community, honored to share its history. Another section of wall depicts the history of the bridges over the Missisquoi River. Some were covered, meant for carts, wagons and horses. Others were built to support the county's now-defunct railroad infrastructure. The society displays native artifacts found along the Missisquoi. This group has impressive momentum.

SWANTON

The Swanton Historical Society manages two locations, both having some significance within the community. Its office space and parts of its collection are located in the Swanton Public Library. Volunteers maintain and organize the collection. They field occasional questions about genealogy and family links to Swanton. The second location is the Ron Kilburn Transportation Museum, the original depot from the area's forgotten rail industry. It is the very spot where Swanton's rail wheelhouse was once located. It is on the banks of the winding Missisquoi River, near the very popular walking bridge. Further eye candy for rail connoisseurs is the old red caboose, prominently displayed not far from the existing railroad tracks. The property features an antique handcar and the original tollhouse that was stationed on the Missisquoi Bay Bridge for decades. The town boasts an impressive history unmatched by many in the state.

ST. ALBANS

The St. Albans Museum and Historical Society is one of the prize organizations for anyone who likes history in the county. Located above Taylor Park in the center of the city, the society has enough space for multiple displays. The first floor has a newly developed focus on the city's railroad history. Long ago, St. Albans was the rail capital of northwestern Vermont, and a new exhibit headlines the stories of workers—the men and women whose labor fueled the industry's success. The first floor also has a first-class military display, which covers everything from the Revolutionary War to modern conflicts. If that isn't enough, the second floor boasts a collection of fashion and clothing styles from the late nineteenth and early twentieth centuries and an impressive Abenaki history display. It appropriately honors the presence of the region's indigenous peoples. Another room features a first-class exhibit honoring education. Old-style teaching techniques are on full display, with hard wood desks and chalkboards. The location is accessible and available to large groups. The society hosts history classes on a regular basis. The third floor is often used as a conference and meeting center. This museum is the largest and most visible preservation effort in the county.

SINCERE APOLOGIES GO TO the Fletcher Historical Society. Efforts to arrange a visit during the COVID-19 pandemic proved problematic. Rest assured, its history is every bit as interesting as what is listed herein.

NOTES

Chapter One

1. Power and Haviland, *Original Vermonters.*
2. Power and Haviland, "Beckoning Country," 20–30.
3. Calloway, *Western Abenaki of Vermont.*
4. Power and Haviland, *Original Vermonters.*
5. Wiseman, "Coming of the Others," 56.
6. Wiseman, "Apothesis of Wabanaki Life," 148–49.
7. Power and Haviland, "Woodland Period in Vermont," 85.
8. Wiseman, "Coming of the Others," 56.
9. Crock, "Exploring the 14th–16th Centuries.
10. Wiseman, "Indigenous Corn of the Far Northeast," 60.
11. Power and Haviland, "Woodland Period in Vermont," 85.
12. Wiseman, "Indigenous Corn of the Far Northeast," 60.
13. Ibid.

Chapter Two

14. Randall, *Ethan Allen.*
15. Barney and Perry, *History of the Town of Swanton.*
16. Baker, "July 25, 1775."
17. Brown, "American Archives."
18. Wells, "Journal of Bayze Wells," 242–48.

19. Northern Illinois Univesity Digitial Library, "1776."

20. Chamberlin, "February 26, 1776."

21. Metcalf, "July 21, 1776."

22. Brownson, "Letter from Captain Brownson to General Gates."

23. Gates, "Letter from General Gates to the President of Congress."

24. Washington, *Carleton's Raid*.

Chapter Three

25. Lampee, "Missisquoi Loyalists."

26. Montgomery, "Missisquoi Bay, Philipsburgh Quebec."

27. Nye, "Loyalists and Their Property," 36–44.

28. Lampee, "Missisquoi Loyalists."

29. Ibid.

30. Montgomery, "Missisquoi Bay, Philipsburgh Quebec."

31. Lampee, "Missisquoi Loyalists."

32. Montgomery, "Missisquoi Bay, Philipsburgh Quebec."

33. Lampee, "Missisquoi Loyalists Part II," 97–112.

34. Ibid.

35. Lampee, "Missisquoi Loyalists."

36. Barney and Perry, *History of the Town of Swanton*.

37. Anderson, "Highgate as Seen from an Old Account Book, Part I."

38. Lampee, "Missisquoi Loyalists."

39. Montgomery, "Missisquoi Bay, Philipsburgh Quebec."

40. Anderson, "Highgate as Seen from an Old Account Book, Part I."

41. Montgomery, "Missisquoi Bay, Philipsburgh Quebec."

42. Lampee, "Missisquoi Loyalists Part IV."

43. Lynch, "4th Annual Report of the Missisquoi County Historical Society."

44. Anderson, "Highgate as Seen from an Old Account Book, Part I," 121–32.

Chapter Four

45. Greer, *Patriots and the People*.

46. Montgomery, "1837 Rebellion," 101–10.

47. Greer, "Queen Is a Whore!"

48. *Vermont Watchman and State Journal*, December 4, 1837.

49. *Burlington Weekly Free Press*, December 1, 1837.

50. *Vermont Gazette*, "Disturbances in Canada."
51. Barney and Perry, "Patriot War," 1070–76.
52. Ibid.
53. Lynch, "4th Annual Report of the Missisquoi County Historical Society."
54. Montgomery, "1837 Rebellion," 101–10.
55. Rootsweb Township Information, "Highgate, Part Two."
56. Lynch, "4th Annual Report of the Missisquoi County Historical Society."
57. Rootsweb Township Information, "Highgate, Part Two."
58. Montgomery, "1837 Rebellion," 101–10.
59. Barney and Perry, "Patriot War," 1070–76.
60. Montgomery, "1837 Rebellion," 101–10.
61. Lynch, "4th Annual Report of the Missisquoi County Historical Society."
62. Barney and Perry, "Enrollment in Platt's Volenteers," 1059, 1060.
63. Lynch, "4th Annual Report of the Missisquoi County Historical Society."
64. Montgomery, "1837 Rebellion," 101–10.
65. Barney and Perry, "Patriot War," 1070–76.
66. Anderson, "Highgate as Seen from an Old Account Book, Part I."

Chapter Five

67. Swanton Historical Society, "Outline of Swanton's History."
68. Ibid.
69. Rootsweb, Township Information, "Bakersfield."
70. Royce, Rootsweb, Township Information, "Berkshire."
71. Adams, Rootsweb, Township Information, "Enosburg."
72. Perley, Rootsweb, Township Information, "Fairfield."
73. Fairfax Historical Society, "Baptist Building of Fairfax."
74. Rootsweb, Township Information, "Fletcher."
75. Vermont Division of Historic Preservation, *Franklin*.
76. Rootsweb Township Information, "Highgate, Part Two."
77. Montgomery Historical Society, "History of Pratt Hall."
78. Branthoover, "History of the Baptist Church."
79. Salisbury, *Richford Vermont, Frontier Town*.
80. Ibid.
81. Ibid.
82. Ibid.
83. Dutcher, Rootsweb, Township Information, "St. Albans."
84. Sheldon Historical Society, "The Sheldon Time Line of History."

Chapter Six

85. Jones, "Central Vermont Railway," 168–227.
86. Salisbury, *Richford Vermont, Frontier Town.*

Chapter Seven

87. Coffin, *Nine Months to Gettysburg.*
88. Myers, "Major Efforts of the Anti-Slavery Agents in Vermont," 214–29.
89. Sturtevant, "13th Regiment Vermont Volunteers."
90. Ibid.
91. Coffin, "Franklin County."
92. Ibid.
93. Sturtevant, "13th Regiment Vermont Voleneers."
94. Coffin, *Nine Months to Gettysburg.*
95. Coffin, "Franklin County."
96. Sturtevant, "13th Regiment Vermont Volunteers."
97. "Guerrilla Raid in Vermont," *Burlington Weekly Free Press.*
98. Sherburne, *Saint Albans Raid.*
99. Johnson, *Saint Albans Raid.*
100. Sherburne, *Saint Albans Raid.*
101. Rootsweb, Township Information, "Highgate, Part Two."
102. "General Orders," *Burlington Daily Times.*
103. Johnson, *Saint Albans Raid.*
104. "Protection Against Future Raids," *Burlington Daily Times.*

Chapter Eight

105. Rootsweb, Township Information, "Bakersfield."
106. "To the Editor," *Saint Albans Weekly Messenger.*
107. "Bakersfield Academy and Literary Association," *Saint Albans Messenger,*
    February 12, 1845.
108. "Bakersfield Academy and Literary Association," *Saint Albans Messenger,*
    May 28, 1846.
109. "Bakersfield Academy," February 14, 1856.
110. "Bakersfield Academy," *Democrat.*
111. "State News," *Burlington Weekly Free Press.*

112. Swanton Historical Society, "An Outline of Swanton's History."

113. *Swanton Courier*, July 25, 1963.

114. "Catholic School May Reopen," *Burlington Free Press*.

115. "Holy Angels Parish to Mark Centenary," *Burlington Free Press*.

Chapter Nine

116. *Saint Albans Daily Messenger*, January 22, 1875.

117. "Ice Men," *Saint Albans Daily Messenger*.

118. "Town Affairs," *Saint Albans Daily Messenger*.

119. "Swanton," *Saint Albans Messenger*, May 21, 1900.

120. Ibid.

121. "North Berkshire," *Saint Albans Messenger*.

122. "Enosburg Falls," *Saint Albans Messenger*.

123. "Ice Harvesting Completed," *Saint Albans Messenger*.

124. "Fletcher," *Saint Albans Messenger*.

125. "West Fletcher," *Saint Albans Daily Messenger*.

126. "Sheldon Springs," *Saint Albans Messenger*.

127. "Highgate Springs," *Saint Albans Messenger*.

128. "Ice 30 Inches Thick," *Saint Albans Messenger*.

129. "New Ice Industry," *Saint Albans Messenger*.

130. "Ice Cutting Notice," *Saint Albans Daily Messenger*.

131. "Ice Only Nine Inches Thick," *Saint Albans Daily Messenger*.

132. "Teams Were Overloaded," *Saint Albans Daily Messenger*.

133. "Injured While Ice Harvesting," *Saint Albans Daily Messenger*.

134. "Berkshire," *Saint Albans Daily Messenger*.

135. "Fairfield," *Saint Albans Daily Messenger*.

136. "Ice From Artifical Lake," *Saint Albans Daily Messenger*.

Chapter Ten

137. "1300 Guardsmen to Leave Fort," *Saint Johnsbury Caledonian*.

138. "Company B Equipped," *Swanton Courier*.

139. "Swanton," *Burlington Free Press*.

140. "Honor for Company B," *Saint Albans Messenger*.

141. "Company B Left Quietly," *Swanton Courier*.

142. "Soldier Shot Near Swanton," *Barre Daily Times*.

143. "Condition of the Sick," *Saint Albans Messenger*.

144. "Detailed to Plattsburgh," *Saint Albans Daily Messenger*.

145. "Swanton," *Burlington Free Press*.

146. "Praise for Company B," *Saint Albans Messenger*.

147. "Investigate Deaths," *Burlington Free Press*.

148. "Company B Is Now up to War Strength," *Swanton Courier*.

149. "Swanton War Plant Blows Up," *Burlington Free Press*.

Chapter Eleven

150. Roos, "Why the Second Wave."

151. Sherman, "Spanish Flu in Vermont."

152. Roos, "Why the Second Wave."

153. "528 Cases of Influenza Here," *Saint Albans Messenger*.

154. "Swanton," *Saint Albans Messenger*, October 1918.

155. "Sheldon," *Saint Albans Messenger*.

156. "Take Notice," *Saint Albans Messenger*, October 11, 1918, 7.

157. "Condition of the Sick," *Saint Albans Messenger*.

158. "Take Notice," *Saint Albans Messenger*, October 15, 1918, 4.

159. "Conditions in Saint Albans Getting Back to Normal," *Saint Albans Messenger*.

160. "Take Notice," *Saint Albans Messenger*, October 21, 1918, 8.

161. "Must Still Be Careful," *Saint Albans Messenger*.

162. "Swanton," *Saint Albans Messenger*, November 8, 1918, 2.

163. "Fairfield," *Saint Albans Messenger*.

164. "Enosburg Falls," *Saint Albans Messenger*, November 1918.

165. "Swanton," *Saint Albans Messenger*.

166. "West Berkshire," *Saint Albans Messenger*.

167. "Ten Cases of Influenza Reported," *Saint Albans Messenger*.

168. "Take Notice," *Saint Albans Messenger*.

169. Sherman, "Spanish Flu in Vermont."

Chapter Twelve

170. "St. Albans Losses," *Saint Albans Messenger*.

171. "Franklin County Has Many Victims," *Saint Albans Messenger*.

172. "All Central Vermont Through Traffic," *Saint Albans Messenger*.

173. "Richford Is Isolated," *Saint Albans Messenger*.
174. "Enosburg Conditions," *Saint Albans Messenger*.
175. "Guardsmen Patrol Streets," *Saint Albans Messenger*.
176. "Richford Is Divided," *Saint Albans Messenger*.
177. "Flood Notes," *Saint Albans Messenger*.
178. "Enosburg Conditions," *Saint Albans Messenger*.
179. "Homeless in Enosburg," *Saint Albans Messenger*.
180. "Bradley Soule in Flooded Area," *Saint Albans Messenger*.
181. "Survery Made of Franklin County," *Saint Albans Messenger*.

Chapter Thirteen

182. *Saint Albans Daily Messenger*, April 5, 1897.
183. *Saint Albans Daily Messenger*, April 29, 1897.
184. Ibid.
185. *Swanton Courier*, September 10, 1897.
186. "Sheldon Junction," *Saint Albans Daily Messenger*.
187. "Swanton," *Saint Albans Daily Messenger*.
188. "East Fairfield," *Saint Albans Daily Messenger*.
189. "East Enosburg," *Saint Albans Daily Messenger*.
190. "America's Greatest Exhibition of Moving Pictures," *Saint Albans Daily Messenger*.
191. "Local Mention," *Richford Journal and Gazette*.
192. "To Build a New Picture Theatre," *Swanton Courier*.
193. *Saint Albans Daily Messenger*, August 30, 1924.

Chapter Fourteen

194. "Notes," *Burlington Free Press*.
195. "Smuggling in Liquor," *Brattleboro Daily Reformer*.
196. "Charged with Smuggling," *Burlington Free Press*.
197. "Suit Cases Held Liquor," *Barre Daily Times*.
198. "Vermont News," *Brattleboro Daily Reformer*, December 23, 1919.
199. "Vermont News," *Brattleboro Daily Reformer*.
200. "Free Rum Running across Border," *Brattleboro Daily Reformer*.
201. "Make Booze Seizure," *Burlington Free Press*.
202. "Deny Smuggling," *Barre Daily Times*.

203. "New Custom's Patrol Boat Launched Yesterday," *Saint Albans Messenger*.

204. "Huge Beer Haul Made by Customs," *Saint Albans Messenger*.

205. "State News," *Landmark*.

206. "Use Canoe to Smuggle Hooch," *Saint Albans Messenger*.

207. "Two Arrests Made—Machines Believed to Be Operating in Pairs," *Saint Albans Messenger*.

208. "Farrar Piano Liquor Cash," *Barre Daily Times*.

209. "Barge of Hay Being Held by Customs Men," *Plattsburg Sentinal*.

210. "Seized Rowboat with 240 Quarts of Ale," *Ticonderoga Sentinal*.

211. "Seize Five Booze Car on Vermont," *Plattsburgh Daily Republican*.

212. "Booze Boat Taken on Lake Champlain," *Plattsburgh Republican*.

213. "Close Navigation on Lake Champlain," *Ticonderoga Sentinal*.

214. "Babcock's Body Still in Lake," *Plattsburgh Daily Press*.

215. "Rumrunner Knocks Officer Into Lake," *Plattsburgh Daily Press*.

Chapter Fifteen

216. Hoffbeck, "Remember the Poor," 225.

217. Ibid.

218. Ibid.

219. "Town Officers Elected," *Saint Albans Daily Messenger*.

220. "Daily Messenger," *Saint Albans Daily Messenger*.

221. Hoffbeck, "Remember the Poor," 225.

222. Ibid

223. "Run Over and Killed," *Saint Albans Messenger*.

224. "Man Who Isn't Sorry," *Saint Albans Daily Messenger*, 1874)

225. "Care and Support of the Poor," *Saint Albans Daily Messenger*, 1868.

226. "Town Reports," *Saint Albans Daily Messenger*.

227. "Bakersfield," *Saint Albans Daily Messenger*.

228. "Town Reports," *Saint Albans Daily Messenger*.

229. "Home Matters," *Saint Albans Daily Messenger*.

230. "Local Business," *Richford Journal and Gazette*, 1886)

231. "Card of Thanks," *Saint Albans Daily Messenger*.

232. Hoffbeck, "Remember the Poor," 225.

233. "Barns Burned," *Saint Albans Daily Messenger*.

234. "Sheldon Springs," *Saint Albans Daily Messenger*.

235. "Disgrace to Humanity," *Saint Albans Daily Messenger*.

236. "Tuberculosis at Sheldon Poor Farm," *Swanton Courier*.

237. "State Notes," *Richford Journal and Gazette*.
238. "Sheldon Springs," *Saint Albans Daily Messenger*.
239. "County Poorhouse Fired by Inmate," *Barre Daily Times*.
240. "Deplorable State," *Enosburgh Standard*.
241. "Small Pox in Sheldon," *Bridport Sun*.
242. "City Briefs," *Rutland Daily Herald*.

Chapter Sixteen

243. "Failed Banks Unsound," *Saint Albans Messenger*.
244. "State News Briefs," *Saint Albans Messenger*.
245. "Bridge Commission Votes to Advance Plan," *Saint Albans Messenger*.
246. "Missisquoi Bay Bridge Commission Puts Plans Together," *Burlington Free Press*.
247. "Job Scheduled to Be Done This Year," *Saint Albans Messenger*.
248. "Saint Albans Sewage Disposal Plant," *Living New Deal*.
249. "Missisquoi Brigde Span to Be Put in Soon," *Burlington Free Press*.
250. "Alburg Man Crushed Under Load of Stone," *Saint Albans Messenger*.
251. "Bridge Commission Needs $66,000 to Complete Structure," *Burlington Clipper*.
252. "Henry P. Jones Dies in Night at St. Albans," *Deerfield Valley Times*.
253. "370,000 Trees Ordered for Planting," *Saint Albans Daily Messenger*.
254. "807,100 Trees Planted in State," *Saint Albans Daily Messenger*.
255. "Merrill Plan," *Saint Albans Messenger*.
256. "Tomorrow's Meeting," *Saint Albans Messenger*.
257. "Visualizes Recreation Spots on Bellevue and at the Bay," *Saint Albans Messenger*.
258. "Inspection Station—West Berkshire, VT," *Living New Deal*.
259. "64 WPA Projects Okayed; None in St. A," *Saint Albans Messenger*.
260. "Council Discusses New WPA Projects," *Saint Albans Messenger*.
261. "High School and Streets for St. A," *Saint Albans Messenger*.
262. "County WPA Jobs Are Given Approval," *Saint Albans Messenger*.
263. "Inspection Station—Franklin, VT," *Living New Deal*.
264. "New Structure on State WPA Program," *Saint Albans Messenger*.
265. "Plans Completed for Work on Dozen School Houses," *Saint Albans Messenger*.
266. "Cost of Living Survey in County," *Saint Albans Messenger*.
267. "Historic Building Fully Restored," *Saint Albans Messenger*.

268. "Post Office (Former) Murals," *Living New Deal*.
269. "Inspection Station (Demolished)—Highgate Springs, VT," *Living New Deal*.
270. "Missisquoi River Dam—Richford, VT," *Living New Deal*.

Chapter Seventeen

271. Sagerman, *Vermont Historic Sites and Structures Survey Report*.
272. Radomes.org, "Information for Saint Albans AFS, VT."
273. Ledoux, "Missile Base Lured Soviet Agent."
274. Ibid.
275. Ibid.

Chapter Eighteen

276. Daley, *Going Up the Country*, 21.
277. Daloz, *We Are as Gods*, 56.
278. Ibid., 76.
279. Ibid.
280. "'Subversive' Paper May Cost UVM Funds," *Burlington Free Press*.
281. Bruce Taub, "To the Town Librarian," *Bruce Taub.net* (blog), February 2016.
282. Andrews, interview.
283. HonorStates.org 2019.
284. Daloz, *We Are as Gods*, 77.
285. Ibid.
286. Ibid.
287. Vietnam Veterans Memorial Fund n.d.
288. *Swanton Courier*, 1971.
289. Meta Strick, interview conducted by the author, 2019.
290. *Saint Albans Messenger*, 1971.
291. "Hippies Wanted to Observe Birth in Great Outdoors," *Saint Albans Messenger*, 1971.
292. "Power Station Posts Sub-Station Guards," *Saint Albans Messenger*, 1971.
293. Davis, *Mocking Justice*.

BIBLIOGRAPHY

Adams, George. "History of the Town of Enosburgh." Rootsweb, Township Information. 2004. Accessed July 25, 2020. https://sites.rootsweb.com.

Anderson, George. "Highgate as Seen from an Old Account Book, Part I." *Vermont History Journal* (Vermont Historical Society) (1939): 121–32.

Andrews, Mary Louise. Interview by Kate Blofsin. 2015. *Vermont Oral History Project* (September 30).

Baker, Remember. "July 25, 1775." Northern Illinois University Digital Library. Accessed September 5, 2020. https://digital.lib.niu.edu.

Barney, George, and John Perry. "Enrollment in Platt's Volunteers." In *The History of the Town of Swanton*, by George Barney and John Perry, 1059, 1060. Swanton, VT: Higginson Book Company, 1882.

———. *The History of the Town of Swanton*. Swanton, VT: Higginson Book Company, 1882.

———. "The Patriot War." In *History of the Town of Swanton*, by George Barney and John Perry, 1070–76. Swanton, VT: Higginson Book Company, 1882.

Barre (VT) Daily Times. "County Poorhouse Fired by Inmate." January 24, 1913, 1.

———. "Deny Smuggling." November 28, 1921.

———. "Farrar Piano Liquor Cash." April 2, 1925, 1.

———. "Soldier Shot Near Swanton." April 24, 1917.

———. "Suit Cases Held Liquor." December 15, 1919.

Branthoover, W.R. "History of the Baptist Church." Montgomery Historical Society. Accessed July 26, 2020. http://montgomeryhistoricalsociety.org.

Brattleboro (VT) Daily Reformer. 1920. "Free Rum Running Across Border."
     September 20.
———. "Smuggling in Liquor." August 22, 1919.
———. "Vermont News." December 23, 1919.
———. "Vermont News." Deccember 26, 1919.
Bridport (VT) Sun. "Small Pox in Sheldon." April 23, 1903, 6.
Brownson, Captain. "Letter from Captain Brownson to General Gates.
     July 14, 1776." Northern Illinois University Digital Library. Accessed
     September 6, 2020. https://digital.lib.niu.edu.
Brown, Major John. "American Archives: Documents of the American
     Revolutionary Period, 1774–1776." Northern Illinois University Digital
     Library. Accessed September 5, 2020. https://digital.lib.niu.edu.
Brymner, Douglas. *Report on the Canadian Archives.* Ottowa, August 29, 1778.
     Accessed September 6, 2020. https://books.google.com.
Burlington (VT) Clipper. "Bridge Commission Needs $66,000 to Complete
     Structure." January 20, 1938, 1.
Burlington (VT) Daily Times. "General Orders." November 8, 1864, 3.
———. "Protection Against Future Raids." October 27, 1864, 3.
Burlington (VT) Free Press. "Catholic School May Reopen to Ease Swanton
     Crunch." November 24, 1977, 20.
———. "Charged with Smuggling." October 6, 1919.
———. "Holy Angels Parish to Mark Centenary." October 28, 1972, 4.
———. "Holy Angels School Expected to Close." April 2, 1976, 9.
———. "Make Booze Seizure." October 21, 1920.
———. "Missisquoi Brigde Span to Be Put in Soon." May 12, 1937, 2.
———. "Investigate Deaths." June 21, 1917.
———. "Notes." April 24, 1919.
———. "'Subversive' Paper May Cost UVM Funds." March 7, 1970, 13.
———. "Swanton." April 12, 1917.
———. "Swanton." May 17, 1917.
———. "Swanton War Plant Blows Up." April 4, 1918.
Burlington (VT) Weekly Free Press. December 1, 1837, 2.
———. "Guerrilla Raid In Vermont." October 27, 1864, 1.
———. "State News." February 29, 1879, 4.
Calloway, Colin G. *The Western Abenaki of Vermont, 1600 to 1800.* Norman:
     University of Oklahoma Press, 1990.
Chamberlin, Silas. "February 26, 1776." Northern Illinois University
     Digital Library. Accessed September 6, 2020. https://digital.lib.niu.edu/
     islandora/search/SIlas%20Chamberlin?type=edismax.

Coffin, Howard. "Franklin County." In *Something Abides*, by Howard Coffin. Woodstock, VT: Countryman Press, 2013.

———. *Nine Months to Gettysburg.* Woodstock, VT: Countryman Press, 1997.

Crock, John. "Exploring the 14th–16th Centuries of Native Settlement in the Champlain Valley." Lecture. Burlington, Vermont, October 9, 2013.

Daley, Yvonne. *Going Up the Country: When the Hippies, Dreamers, Freaks, and Radicals Moved to Vermont.* Hanover, NH: University Press of New England, 2018.

Daloz, Kate. *We Are as Gods: Back to the Land in the 1970s on the Quest for a New America.* New York: Public Affairs, 2016.

Davis, Hamilton E. *Mocking Justice.* Shelburne, VT: New England Press, 1978.

Deerfield Valley Times. "Henry P. Jones Dies in Night at St. Albans." February 11, 1938, 1.

Democrat (Brattleboro, VT). "Bakersfield Academy." August 9, 1859, 3.

Dutcher, L.L. "St. Albans." Rootsweb, Township Information. Accessed July 27, 2020. https://sites.rootsweb.com.

Enosburg (VT) Standard. 1927. "Deplorable State at Sheldon Poor Farm." November 18: 1.

Fairfax Historical Society. "The Baptist Building of Fairfax." April 29, 2000. Accessed July 23, 2020. http://www.vtgrandpa.com.

Gates, Horatio. "Letter from General Gates to the President of Congress. August 6, 1776." Northern Illinois University Digital Library. Accessed September 6, 2020. https://digital.lib.niu.edu.

Georgia Historical Society. "Georgia United Methodist Church." Georgia Historical Society. Accessed July 23, 2020. https://georgiahistoricalsocietyvt.org.

Greer, Alan. "The Queen Is a Whore!" In *The Patriots and the People*, by Alan Greer, 189–218. Toronto: Toronto University Press, 1993.

———. "Rural Society and Agrarian Economy." In *The Patriots and the People*, by Alan Greer, 20–52. Toronto: University of Toronto Press, 1993.

Hoffbeck, Steven R. "Remember the Poor: Poor Farms in Vermont." *Vermont Historical Journal* (Vermont Historical Society) 57, no. 4 (1989): 225.

Johnson, Carl E. 2001. *The Saint Albans Raid: 19 October 1864.* Saint Albans, VT: self-published, 2001.

Jones, Robert. 1993. "Central Vermont Railway." In *Railroads of Vermont, Vol. I*, by Robert C. Jones, 168–227. Shelburne, VT: New England Press.

Kade, Barry. Interview by Jason Barney. 2019. *Online Interview, Franklin County Communes* (October 21–24).

Kalinoski, Sarah V. "Sequestration, Confiscation, and the 'Tory' in the Vermont Revolution." *Vermont History Journal* (1977): 236–46.

Kingsley, Ben. "History of the Town of Fletcher." Rootsweb, Township Information. 1871. Accessed July 24, 2020. https://sites.rootsweb.com.

Lampee, Thomas. "The Missisquoi Loyalists." *Vermont History Journal* (1938): 89–96.

———. "The Missisquoi Loyalists Part IV." *Vermont History Journal* (1938).

———. "The Missisquoi Loyalists, Part III." *Vermont History Journal* (1938): 113–27.

———. "Missisquoi Loyalists Part II." *Vermont History Journal* (1938): 97–112.

Landmark (White River Junction, VT). "State News." June 25, 1925, 2.

Ledoux, Rod. "Missile Base Lured Soviet Agent." *Saint Albans Messenger*, 1967.

Living New Deal. "Inspection Station (Demolished)—Highgate Springs, VT." Accessed July 13, 2020. https://livingnewdeal.org.

———. "Inspection Station—Franklin, VT." Accessed July 13, 2020. https://livingnewdeal.org.

———. "Inspection Station—West Berkshire, VT." Accessed July 13, 2020. https://livingnewdeal.org.

———. "Missisquoi River Dam—Richford, VT." Accessed July 13, 2020. https://livingnewdeal.org.

———. "Post Office (Former) Murals—Saint Albans, VT." Accessed July 13, 2020. https://livingnewdeal.org.

———. "Saint Albans Sewage Disposal Plant—Saint Albans, VT." Accessed July 13, 2020. https://livingnewdeal.org.

Lynch, W.W. 1909. "St. Armand Negro Burying Ground." In *The 4th Annual Report of the Missisquoi County Historical Society*, by W.W. Lynch, 62–63. St. John's, Canada: News Type.

Lynch, W.W. "The 4th Annual Report of the Missisquoi County Historical Society." In *Report on the Transactions of the Missisquoi Historical Society*. Quebec, Canada: News Print, 1909.

Metcalf, Simon. "July 21, 1776." Northern Illinois University Digital Library. Accessed September 6, 2020. https://digital.lib.niu.edu.

Montgomery Historical Society. "History of Pratt Hall." Accessed July 26, 2020. http://montgomeryhistoricalsociety.org.

Montgomery, George H. "The 1837 Rebellion." In *Missisquoi Bay, Philipsburgh Quebec*, by George Montgomery. Granby, Quebec: Grandby Printing and Publishing, 1950.

———. "Missisquoi Bay, Philipsburgh Quebec." In *Missisquoi Bay, Philipsburgh Quebec*, by George H. Montgomery, 17–42. Granby, Quebec: Grandby Printing and Publishing, 1950.

Myers, John. "The Major Efforts of the Anti-Slavery Agents in Vermont, 1836–1838." *Vermont History Journal* (1968): 214–29.

Northern Illinois Univesity Digitial Library. "June 28, 1776." Accessed September 5, 2020. https://digital.lib.niu.edu.

Nye, Mary Green. "Loyalists and Their Property." *Vermont Historical Journal* (1942): 36–44.

Perley, Samuel. Rootsweb, Township Information. "History of the Town of Fairfield." Accessed July 24, 2020. 1871. http://sites.rootsweb.com.

Plattsburgh (NY) Daily Press. "Babcock's Body Still In Lake." August 19, 1931.

———. "Rumrunner Knocks Officer into Lake with Baseball Bat." August 13, 1932.

Plattsburgh (NY) Daily Republican. "Seize Five Booze Car on Vermont." September 4, 1928.

Plattsburgh (NY) Republican. "Booze Boat Taken on Lake Champlain With 480 Bottles." June 8, 1929.

Plattsburg (NY) Sentinal. "Barge of Hay Being Held By Customs Men." August 19, 1927: 6.

Power, Marjory, and William Haviland. "The Beckoning Country." In *The Original Vermonters*, by Marjory Power and William Haviland, 20–30. Hanover, NH: University Press of New England, 1994.

———. *The Original Vermonters*. Hanover, NH: University Press of New England, 1994.

———. "The Woodland Period in Vermont." In *The Original Vermonters*, by Marjory Power and William Haviland, 85. Hanover, NH: University Press of New England, 1994.

Radomes.org. "Information for Saint Albans AFS, VT." Accessed June 2, 2020. https://www.radomes.org.

Randall, Willard. *Ethan Allen: His Life and Times*. New York: Norton, 2011.

Richford (VT) Journal and Gazette. "Local Mention." January 8, 1907, 3.

———. "State Notes." February 7, 1907, 2.

Roos, Dave. "Why the Second Wave of the 1918 Flu Pandemic Was So Deadly." History.com. Accessed July 22, 2020. https://www.history.com.

Rootsweb, Township Information. "Bakersfield." Accessed July 25, 2020. https://sites.rootsweb.com.

Rootsweb, Township Information. "Highgate, Part Two." Accessed July 25, 2020. https://sites.rootsweb.com.

Royce, Stephen. 2004. "History of the Town of Berkshire." Rootsweb, Township Information. Accessed July 25, 2020. http://sites.rootsweb.com.

Rutland (VT) Daily Herald. "City Briefs." November 25, 1907, 8.

Sagerman, Paula. "National Guard Buildings." *Vermont Historic Sites and Structures Survey Report: Vermont National Guard*. Wilmington, VT: Vermont Department of Historic Preservation, 2009.

Saint Albans (VT) Daily Messenger, April 29, 1897, 5.

———. "America's Greatest Exhibition of Moving Pictures." September 4, 1904, 7.

———. August 30, 1924, 3.

———. "Bakersfield." November 3, 1875, 2.

———. "Berkshire." February 19, 1919, 6.

———. "Care and Support of the Poor." May 13, 1865.

———. "Condition of the Sick." April 30, 1917, 2.

———. "Daily Messenger." January 6, 1874.

———. "Detailed to Plattsburgh." May 19, 1917, 1.

———. "East Enosburg." November 26, 1901, 6.

———. "East Fairfield." October 25, 1901, 6.

———. "807,100 Trees Planted in State." September 16, 1932, 4.

———. "Fairfield." January 24, 1916, 2.

———. "Home Matters." January 24, 1882.

———. "Ice Cutting Notice." December 13, 1913, 7.

———. "Ice from Artifical Lake." January 15, 1917, 8.

———. "The Ice Men." February 9, 1892, 3.

———. "Ice Only Nine Inches Thick." February 5, 1913, 2.

———. "Injured While Ice Harvesting." February 13, 1913, 7.

———. January 31, 1874.

———. January 22, 1875, 3.

———. May 21, 1897, 4.

———. "Sheldon Junction." March 7, 1900, 2.

———. "Sheldon Springs." July 8, 1910, 4.

———. "Swanton." May 21, 1900, 4.

———. "Swanton." October 2, 1918, 8.

———. "Teams Were Overloaded." March 6, 1913, 8.

———. "370,000 Trees Ordered For Planting." March 4, 1932, 4.

———. "Town Affairs." February 10, 1892, 4.

———. "Town Officers Elected." March 5, 1875, 3.

———. "Town Reports." February 28, 1879.

———. "Town Reports." February 23, 1874, 3.

———. "West Fletcher." March 13, 1916, 5.

Saint Albans (VT) Messenger. "Alburg Man Crushed Under Load of Stone." November 23, 1937, 1.

———. "All Central Vermont Through Traffic Is at a Standstill." November 4, 1927, 1.

———. "Bakersfield Academy." February 14, 1856, 3.

———. "Bakersfield Academy and Literary Association." February 12, 1845, 3.

———. "Bakersfield Academy and Literary Association." May 28, 1846, 3.

———. "Bradley Soule in Flooded Area." November 7, 1927, 2.

———. "Bridge Commission Votes to Advance Plan." August 8, 1934, 8.

———. "Condition of the Sick." October 15, 1918, 8.

———. "Conditions in Saint Albans Getting Back to Normal." October 19, 1918, 1.

———. "Cost of Living Survey in County." June 5, 1936, 3.

———. "Council Discusses New WPA Projects." September 10, 1935, 7.

———. "County WPA Jobs Are Given Approval." August 30, 1935, 7.

———. "Enosburg Conditions." November 5, 1927, 2.

———. "Enosburg Conditions." November 4, 1927, 2.

———. "Enosburg Falls." January 25, 1907, 2.

———. "Enosburg Falls." November 22, 1918, 8.

———. "Failed Banks Unsound." January 1933, 4.

———. "Fairfield." November 16, 1918, 7.

———. "528 Cases of Influenza Here." September 30, 1918, 1, 7.

———. "Fletcher." January 16, 1908, 6.

———. "Flood Notes." November 5, 1927, 2.

———. "Franklin County Has Many Victims." November 4, 1927, 1.

———. "Guardsmen Patrol Streets." November 5, 1927, 1.

———. "Highgate Springs." January 15, 1914, 4.

———. "High School and Streets for St. A." August 26, 1935, 1.

———. "Historic Building Fully Restored." November 27, 1937, 1.

———. "Homeless in Enosburg." November 7, 1927, 1.

———. "Honor for Company B." March 31, 1917, 5.

———. "Huge Beer Haul Made By Customs." July 26, 1924, 1.

———. "Ice Harvesting Completed." March 18, 1907, 2.

———. "Ice 30 Inches Thick." February 25, 1914, 7.

———. "Job Scheduled to Be Done This Year." May 16, 1936, 1.

———. March 10, 1897, 5.

———. "The Merrill Plan." September 23, 1933, 4.

———. "Missisquoi Bay Bridge Commission Puts Plans Together." March 21, 1935, 1.

———. "Must Still Be Careful." November 5, 1918, 4.

———. "New Custom's Patrol Boat Launched Yesterday." July 16, 1924, 8.

————. "The New Ice Industry." January 26, 1912, 5.
————. "New Structure on State WPA Program." September 13, 1935, 1.
————. "North Berkshire." January 23, 1907, 2.
————. "Plans Completed for Work on Dozen School Houses." December 23, 1935, 7.
————. "Praise for Company B." May 25, 1917, 8.
————. "Richford Is Divided." November 5, 1927, 2.
————. "Richford Is Isolated." November 4, 1927, 1.
————. "Run Over and Killed." October 15, 1873, 3.
————. "Sheldon." October 7, 1918, 7.
————. "Sheldon Springs." January 13, 1912, 3.
————. "64 WPA Projects Okayed; None in St. A." July 22, 1935, 1.
————. "St. Albans Losses." November 4, 1927, 1.
————. "State News Briefs." February 12, 1932, 4.
————. "Survery Made of Franklin County." November 7, 1927, 1.
————. "Swanton." December 18, 1918, 7.
————. "Swanton." January 14, 1903, 3.
————. "Swanton." January 16, 1903, 6.
————. "Swanton." November 8, 1918, 2.
————. "Take Notice." December 31, 1918, 8.
————. "Take Notice." October 11, 1918, 7.
————. "Take Notice." October 14, 1918, 7.
————. "Take Notice." October 21, 1918, 7.
————. "Ten Cases of Influenza Reported over Weekend." December 30, 1918, 8.
————. "Tomorrow's Meeting." October 25, 1933, 4.
————. "Two Arrests Made—Machines Believed to Be Operating in Pairs." August 28, 1924, 8.
————. "Use Canoe to Smuggle Hooch." September 11, 1925, 7.
————. "Visualizes Recreation Spots on Bellevue and at the Bay." June 21, 1934, 1.
————. "West Berkshire." December 1918, 6.
Saint Albans (VT) Weekly Messenger. "To the Editor." December 25, 1844, 2.
Saint Johnsbury (VT) Caledonian. "1300 Guardsmen to Leave Fort." August 21, 1917, 1.
Salisbury, Jack C. *Richford Vermont, Frontier Town.* Caanan, NH: Phoenix Publishing, 2006. First published, 1987.
Sheldon Historical Society. "The Sheldon Time Line of History." Accessed July 23, 2020. http://sheldonvthistorical.org.

Sherburne, Michelle. 2014. *The Saint Albans Raid*. Charleston, SC: The History Press.

Sherman, Michael. "Spanish Flu in Vermont." In *Historic Roots* 3, no. 1 (1998): 11–17. Vermont Council on the Humanities.

———. *Vermont History*. "The Flu Epidemic. 1918." Accessed July 22, 2020. https://vermonthistory.org.

Sturtevant, Ralph. "The 13th Regiment Vermont Volunteers." In *Historical and Biographical History of the 13th Regiment of Vermont Volunteers*, by Ralph Sturtevant and Carmi Marsh, 33. N.p., 1910.

Swanton (VT) Courier. "Company B Equipped." April 5, 1917, 3.

———. "Company B Is Now Up to War Strength." July 12, 1917, 7.

———. "Company B Left Quietly." April 12, 1917, 3.

———. July 25, 1963, 36.

———. September 10, 1897, 3.

———. "Sheldon Springs." November 9, 1911, 3.

———. "To Build a New Picture Theatre." May 3, 1917.

———. "Tuberculosis at Sheldon Poor Farm." September 13, 1900, 3.

Swanton Historical Society. "An Outline of Swanton's History." Accessed July 28, 2020. http://www.swantonhistoricalsociety.org.

Ticonderoga Sentinal. "Close Navigation on Lake Champlain Friday." December 5, 1929.

———. "Seized Rowboat with 240 Quarts of Ale." August 2, 1928.

Vermont Division of Historic Preservation. *Franklin*. Montpelier, VT: Historic Sites Survey, 1983.

Vermont Gazette. "Disturbances in Canada." November 28, 1837, 2.

Vermont Watchman and State Journal, December 4, 1837, 2.

Washington, Ida. *Carleton's Raid*. Weybridge, VT: Cherry Tree Books, 1977.

Wells, Bayze. "Journal of Bayze Wells." *Connecticut Historical Society Volume VII* (1989): 242–48.

Wiseman, Fred. "The Apothesis of Wabanaki Life." In *Reclaiming the Ancestors*, by Fred Wiseman, 148–49. Hanover, NH: University Press of New England, 2005.

———. "The Coming of the Others." In *The Voice of the Dawn*, by Fred Wiseman, 56. Hanover, NH: University Press of New England, 2001.

———. "Indigenous Corn of the Far Northeast." In *The Seven Sisters*, by Frederick Wiseman, 60. Thomasburg, Canada: Earth Haven Learning Center, 2018.

ABOUT THE AUTHOR

Jason Barney grew up in northern Vermont and received a public school education. His interest in history started at Highgate Elementary when he was just a kid. While he loved social studies classes at an early age, he also fondly remembers his father and grandfather keeping binders on family genealogy. What started out as an intense interest in the American Civil War and World War II turned into a love of high school history classes. He looks back on his time at Missisquoi Valley Union High School and knows that that is when his desire to be a teacher began.

Jason graduated from high school in 1993 and attended the College of Saint Joseph's in Rutland, Vermont. The history courses in college were more in-depth, more detailed and a lot of fun. Jason completed the necessary requirements to become a teacher.

Prior to embracing a career in education, Jason ran for public office. Between 1997 and 2002, he represented the towns of Franklin and Highgate in the Vermont legislature. When he left, he had attained the position of vice-chairman of the Education Committee.

From there, he moved into teaching. He has taken up the mantle from his own wonderful teachers and has been in front of classrooms for eighteen years. The longer he teaches, the more he likes it. His intense interest in local history has allowed him to become president of the Swanton Historical Society.

Presently, Jason lives in St. Albans, Vermont, with his wife, Christine Eldred, and his son, Samuel. They own three acres not too far from Lake

Champlain. Jason loves to garden, read, write and teach. He is a huge *Star Trek* fan and maintains the *Star Trek Timeline*, which has been published multiple times by Pocket Books. He is forty-five years old.

Jason's first book, *Northern Vermont in the War of 1812*, was published by The History Press in 2018.